Simple Ayurve

108 Dhal Recipes

Myra Lewin

Foreword

I decided to compile this little book to show that Ayurvedic principles are universal. They can apply anywhere in the world — to all kinds of cuisines, environments and ingredients.

Ayurveda as the science of living is holistic in nature. It considers us as a part of the world around us. Ayurveda offers us the simple idea that we thrive when we connect to the natural flow of life force, or prana. And this applies no matter where you are on the planet.

A holistic approach to life requires an understanding that everything affects everything else. What this means when it comes to food, is that a balance of the qualities present in what we eat will bring balance into us. Likewise, an imbalance of the qualities in what we eat will create imbalance in our bodies and minds. Food is either our poison or our best medicine.

So I offer you 108 simple recipes to inspire you to prepare food that is medicinal and healing. With these recipes, inspired from global cuisines, you can prepare legumes in an interesting, easy-to-digest manner that brings nourishment to your body and a smile to your face.

Many blessings,

Myra

Myra Lewin

Contents

The book of dhal

Maybe you've heard of the Book of Tao — the *Tao Te Ching*. This classic philosophical text of Chinese Taoism teaches ways to live in the world with integrity and rest in the awareness of the present moment.

This is the book of dhal. And similarly it will guide you to create a connection with your Self in the here and now. As you cook with presence, watch the magic unfold in your kitchen and at your dinner table.

Have fun with these recipes. Let it be an adventure. You never know exactly what will happen in life but if you open your mind and heart you experience results beyond your imagination. Let your food be an expression of love and delight.

The mystical power
of 108

The number 108 has long been considered auspicious in India. It's a multiple of 9, and all multiples of 9 when added together eventually reduce to 9. For example,

$$108: \quad 1+0+8 \; = \; 9$$
$$99: \quad 9+9 \; = \; 18. \; \text{then} \; 1+8 \; = \; 9$$

If you own mala beads you probably know that there is great power in chanting mantra 108 times, and perhaps you have always wondered why. The number 108 seems to be woven into the very fabric of our universe — into astronomy, language, and subtle vibration.

The vedas tell us that the distance between the earth and the sun is 108 times the diameter of the sun, and the distance between the earth and the moon is 108 times the diameter of the moon.

108 is also a key element of the Sanskrit language. There are 54 letters in the Sanskrit alphabet, and each letter is said to have masculine and feminine qualities — a dual vibration. If you multiply 54 by 2, you have 108.

It goes on! Observe the sri yantra, a powerful meditation tool, considered to be the mother of all mandalas. There are 54 points in the sacred symbol where lines intersect, and each intersection is also said to have a dual energy of masculine and feminine, bringing us once again to 108. At the centre of the sri yantra is a bindu — a point that symbolizes the source of creative manifestation.

Creative manifestation

This is what we are doing in the kitchen, isn't it? We have an idea about what to cook and then we bring it into manifestation in order to nourish and heal ourselves. Cooking can be a creative and satisfying process that connects us with nature's abundance.

The preparation and consumption of food can also be regarded as a sacred ritual. The food we eat becomes us: body, mind, and spirit. It forms our very being. Cooking and eating are beautiful ways to connect to our bodies and to nature. If we remember this each time we step into the kitchen, we begin to see amazing results: mental peace, physical health and a greater ability to experience joy in life.

But for many the cooking process doesn't feel creative or reverent. Inspiration doesn't always come easily, and cooking becomes just another task on the to-do list. This attitude towards cooking often goes hand-in-hand with a disconnection from nature and our role in the natural process of life. This is when cooking becomes habitual and repetitive. We rely too heavily on recipes and past ways of doing things, and then boredom sets in. When we are bored we are more inclined to seek pleasure and entertainment in rajasic, stimulating food or tamasic, empty and toxic food choices — all of which leads us away from the sattvic, peaceful mind that is our natural state.

If this sounds like you — often uninspired and dissatisfied with your cooking — know that you need not be bored with what you eat. Make food preparation a priority in your day and enjoy each step in the process. Get to know your local food producers. Take time to gather quality ingredients. Make a meal plan for the week, or at least a couple of days ahead. Get in touch with your intuition and use it alongside your intellect. Then you can creatively manifest beautiful meals every day and lovingly care for your health.

Recipes are just guidelines for ideas. Consider yourself as a creator each time you go into the kitchen. Use your intuition to manifest something new, reflective of that very moment. Recreating from the past can not work well because there are so many factors that affect the cooking process. For example, the temperature in the room, the type of cooktop or oven, the type of cookware being used, the grind of the spices or flour, the age of the beans, and so on. Even the attitude of the cook at the time of cooking will influence the quality of the food created. If you don't like the results you get, then make an adjustment and go for it again. Make it an exploration, not a performance, and have fun! Mistakes are a wonderful opportunity to practice laughing and not taking yourself too seriously.

Allow this simple recipe book to be your guide as you redefine your relationship with food and creativity. Here you'll find 108 great ways to make a nourishing, easy-to-digest mung bean dhal, inspired by cuisines from around the world. We already know that 108 is a sacred number, and mung beans are considered special in Ayurveda too (more on that later). As you explore the recipes, I hope you have a sense that there are an infinite number of possibilities available even when working with one simple main ingredient. Each creation can offer a unique taste and overall effect on your body and mind.

Food as medicine

What is a dhal?

Let's start at the beginning. What is a dhal?

Originating in India, dhal often refers to a split legume. Dhal is also a traditional dish made from well-cooked and spiced legumes. In Ayurveda, dhals are typically made from split or whole mung beans because they are lighter than other legumes, easier to digest and therefore more nourishing. Dhal can also be made from other split legumes such as urad dhal, chana dhal, toor dhal, split peas or red lentils, but these pulses differ in their digestibility and nutrients.

The holistic effect of food

We can understand more about the effects of food and drink on the body by considering the concepts of **rasa, virya** and **vipaka**. The digestive process begins when you put food into your mouth. The first thing that happens is recognition of the primary taste, which is called **rasa**.

The next step is a feeling of warmth or cooling in the stomach and the small intestines. This is the **virya**, the energy that will either fuel or dampen your digestive fire, known as agni. This impact of virya is more obvious when you eat cold things, like ice cream, or hot-spicy things like chilis. But if you bring awareness to the digestive impact of all of the food you eat, you can begin to ascertain the virya of different foods, herbs, oils and spices.

Vipaka is the post-digestive effect of a food or drink that occurs in the colon. The vipaka can affect the elimination of urine, feces and sweat. In general, the rasa, or taste of food dictates the vipaka and the quality of elimination. The sweet, sour and salty rasa will tend to support elimination because of the presence of the water and fire elements. On the other hand, the bitter, pungent and astringent rasa will reduce elimination because of the presence of the dry air and ethers elements.

Ayurveda acknowledges your uniqueness as an individual and considers that experience is subjective. From this standpoint, you can understand that different people may have a different experience of rasa, virya, and vipaka. These things aren't set in stone, and the point is not to get it right. Rather, considering rasa, virya, and vipaka will guide you to tune into your digestion and your body, and form a deeper connection between what you eat and how you feel. Notice your experience of mung beans and how it varies as you cook with different spices and oils.

Rasa: the six tastes

Ayurveda recognizes six distinct tastes, or rasa, in food: sweet, sour, salty, bitter, pungent, and astringent. These tastes are made up of the five elements in nature: earth, water, fire, air and ethers. The three doshas are also made up of these elements. Vata is air and ethers; pitta is fire and water; and kapha is earth and water. When you consume any one of the six tastes, you take in their associated elements which affects the doshas. The tastes also have an effect on your emotions and your attitude in life, as outlined below.

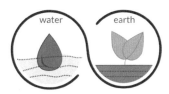

Kapha Dosha (water + earth)

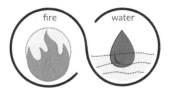

Pitta Dosha (fire + water)

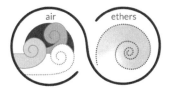

Vata Dosha (air + ethers)

The sweet taste

Qualities: heavy, moist, cool
Impact on Dosha: decreases vata and pitta and increases kapha

In Ayurveda the sweet taste indicates that the food is nourishing to the tissues of the body on all levels. Keep in mind that the Ayurvedic definition of sweet refers to foods that are rejuvenating and pleasant, not sugary. Rice, ghee, milk, ripe fruit, carrots, beets, and sweet potatoes are examples of foods with sweet as their primary taste. The sweet taste nourishes the body and mind and brings resilience and satisfaction. However, too much sweet taste in your food leads to greed and complacency.

The sour taste

Qualities: heavy, moist, warm
Impact on Dosha: decreases vata and increases kapha and pitta

Lemons, cheese, fermented foods, yogurt, and tart apples are examples of the sour taste. An appropriate amount of the sour taste encourages elimination and improves appetite and digestion. Psychologically, it improves discrimination and ability to use the intellect. In excess, the sour taste leads to external evaluation and eventually to jealousy and envy.

The salty taste

Qualities: heavy, moist, warm
Impact on Dosha: decreases vata and increases kapha and pitta

Sea vegetables such as kombu, hijiki and arame are good sources of the salty taste, and of course it is found primarily in natural rock and sea salts. It assists with elimination and softens body tissue leading to flexibility and suppleness. It is grounding to the mind, reduces fear, and encourages enthusiasm for life. However, too much of the salty taste leads to rigidity, bravado, craving, and indulgence in sensory pleasures.

The bitter taste

Qualities: light, dry, cold
Impact on Dosha: decreases pitta and kapha and increases vata

The bitter taste is prominent in leafy greens, endive, eggplant, bitter melon and coffee. Purifying and drying, it helps return all tastes to a balanced place. It also increases appetite and is an anti-aphrodisiac. In appropriate amounts, the bitter taste is sobering and promotes spiritual growth. However, too much of the bitter taste leads to discontent, disillusionment, a bitter attitude, dissatisfaction, and an inability to grow.

The pungent taste

Qualities: light, dry, hot
Impact on Dosha: increases pitta and decreases kapha and vata

Garlic, hot peppers, radishes, mustard greens and ginger are examples of the pungent taste. It improves appetite and encourages the body to let go of secretions such as breast milk, semen, and fat. The appropriate amount encourages extroversion and transformation. However, too much of the pungent taste leads to impatience, passion, intensity, and anger.

The astringent taste

Qualities: light, dry, cool
Impact on Dosha: decreases kapha and pitta and increases vata

Legumes, cruciferous vegetables, cranberries, and rye have significant astringency, which is healing, purifying, and constricting in the body. It reduces secretions and is an anti-aphrodisiac. The astringent taste leads to introversion, the appropriate amount of which promotes equanimity. However, too much introversion makes you closed off, constricted, dull, and insecure. You become dried up, so to speak.

Ideally, all of the six tastes would be included in each meal, but that **does not mean it's a good idea to have an equal amount of each taste in the meal.** You only need a little of the sour and pungent tastes, for example, to bring balance to the whole dish. The tendency when you are out of balance is to crave one or two tastes, leading you to overdo those tastes and forget the others. Following cravings for just one or two tastes will contribute to further imbalance of the doshas.

Remember, also, that Ayurveda is a science based in nature, and you want to consume each rasa from a natural source. It is not the Ayurvedic approach to add refined sugar or processed salt to balance the tastes. Each of the six tastes are present in nature, and can be found in whole grains, vegetables, fruits, herbs, oils and spices.

The concepts that **"like attracts like and the opposite qualities bring balance"** are key Ayurvedic principles that guide you to balance the doshas. A common misconception about Ayurveda is that you must completely eliminate the tastes that increase your primary dosha(s). This is an extreme approach that will lead to a state of imbalance over time. The goal of Ayurveda is to move toward your individual state of balance, your prakruti, and you do this by using all six tastes in moderation. This simple approach will work for most people.

The 6 Tastes

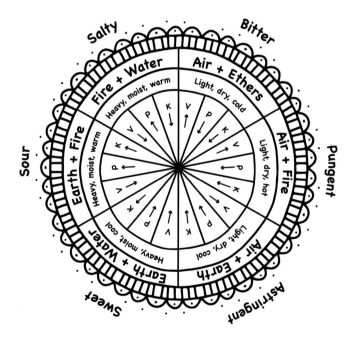

How to be satiated

A balanced meal that integrates all six tastes will not only support digestion, it will taste delicious and leave you feeling satisfied. This balance of the tastes signals to your body that all five elements in nature are present in the meal in an appropriate amount. As stated already, this doesn't mean that the five elements must be present in equal proportion. For example, the fire element is present and strong in the salty and sour tastes. Overdoing these tastes brings imbalance through excess heat in the body and mind. However, when salty and sour tastes are cooked into a meal in small, appropriate amounts, they are supportive of digestion and elimination. Taken together with the other four tastes you will feel satiated and content.

*Augmenting
and extractive foods*

Another powerful concept to guide your balanced meal preparation is to understand that foods have either augmenting or extractive properties. Augmenting foods contain more of the sweet, sour, and salty tastes and add to the body. Extractive foods contain more of the bitter, pungent, and astringent tastes and cleanse or draw things out of the body.

Augmenting foods

Augmenting foods are nourishing, nurturing, and grounding. They replenish and build tissue, and enhance vitality. Examples of augmenting foods are: most whole grains such as rice, steel cut oats, wheat and barley; most grounding, sweet vegetables such as sweet potatoes, carrots, and squash; fresh, organic dairy; and to a lesser extent, fruits. Eating augmenting foods is necessary to maintain the physical body. They renew what is lost, providing you what you need to maintain your body and take action in the world.

Extractive foods

Extractive foods are cleansing in nature because they draw metabolic toxins out of the digestive tract. The body uses essential fats to digest extractive foods which results in a feeling of lightness in the body. So that you stay grounded and nourish your tissues, it's important to have less extractive foods than augmenting foods within each meal. Legumes, nuts, and vegetables with the bitter, astringent, and pungent tastes such as dark leafy greens are examples of extractive foods.

There are some poor-quality foods that do not fit into these general categories. These are typically processed and unnatural foods that contain predominantly sweet, sour, or salty tastes, but are in fact extractive because of the energy that it takes to digest them. Examples are heavily refined foods, junk foods, or anything else difficult to digest. Although considered extractive, these foods are not cleansing in nature because of their poor quality and the challenge they present to the digestion. They ask the body to give up energy and sometimes body tissue to process them. This is why it is essential to use only natural foods when balancing the six tastes in your meal. Ayurvedic cooking is based on the natural intelligence of plants and the five elements contained within them; when we refine foods, we lose this natural intelligence and the connection to nature. Meat is another example of an extractive food that is difficult to digest and does not offer the cleansing action of plant-based extractive foods.

Very simply, meals that include about 60% augmenting food and 40% extractive food will maintain the body and keep the mind balanced. If there is excess weight then 55% augmenting and 45% extractive could be indicated for a short period. If there is emaciation, then 70-80% augmenting and 20-30% extractive would be indicated until body tissue is restored. Growing children also require

70-90% augmenting foods. These percentages are guidelines; it is not necessary or recommended to measure, weigh, or count things out. Getting out of your thinking mind and using your intuition will yield the best results and give a light and easy experience in the kitchen.

Too much extractive food, and not enough high-quality augmenting food leads to imbalance in the doshas and weakens agni, the digestive fire. Extremes in either direction, over time, will lead to disease. Balanced meals are truly satisfying, and eliminate food cravings and the need for snacking. Digestion will become smooth, easy, and efficient, and you will feel replenished, light, and increasingly more comfortable in your body. The simplest meal can be delightful.

*Balanced meals
the 60:40 ratio*

This book offers 108 simple mung bean dhal recipes, but it is not recommended to eat dhal by itself. As a legume predominant in the astringent taste, dhal is extractive and eating only extractive food will slow digestion and elimination.

A complete, balanced meal contains four components that come together in the 60:40 proportion of augmenting and extractive foods. Here are the four components and how much of the plate they should take up:

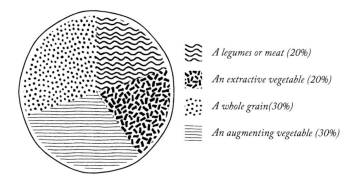

A legumes or meat (20%)

An extractive vegetable (20%)

A whole grain(30%)

An augmenting vegetable (30%)

You can find lists of augmenting and extractive foods at the end of this book to give you the idea. Use the list as a jumping off point, and soon you will learn to identify if a food is augmenting or extractive based on the taste and the experience in your body.

How to choose your whole grain

Good whole grains include rice, pearl barley, millet, wheat, amaranth, rye, teff, and quinoa. These choices are more nourishing and easier to digest than refined grains such as pasta or couscous. Many people shy away from making whole grains because of the length of time required to cook them. If you soak grains the night before or even a few hours before cooking, the cooking time reduces to less than half. You can also reduce the cooking time by using a pressure cooker.

Another augmenting food that pairs nicely with dhal and comes together quickly is whole grain flatbread, like chapati. Unleavened bread is much easier to digest than store-bought breads or breads made with yeast, sourdough or other leavening, which imbalances the doshas.

Many cultures have their own version of flatbread passed down through their heritage like roti (India), tortilla (Latin America), kitcha (Ethiopia), bannock (British Isles), arepa (Columbia/ Venezuela), arboud (Arab Bedouin), reiska (Finland), and bataw (Egypt).

Cooking oils

Using oil when cooking dhal (and most foods) is important as it will improve the digestibility and taste.

There are many nice, high-quality oils like olive oil, coconut oil, and sesame oil. These are fine to consume and contribute to the balance of tastes in a meal, but they are more challenging for agni. Ghee is suggested in most of these recipes as it is the most supportive of agni.

Ghee: liquid sunshine

Ghee is an ancient and sattvic food, highly recommended in Ayurveda for its nourishing qualities and ability to support the absorption of the nutrients of food and herbs deeper into the body tissues. Ghee is tridoshic, meaning it is healing for all doshas and is not congestive like butter. It also improves the skin quality, increases physical and mental stamina, soothes the nerves and lubricates the joints. Although you may find ghee in a store, it is more rewarding, better tasting and less expensive to make at home. Store it at room temperature and out of direct sunlight. Always use a clean, dry utensil for serving; water or foreign particles in the ghee will cause mold.

A simple ghee recipe

Making ghee while the moon is waxing or full is ideal. The moon's soma, or healing energy, is highest during these times and will be present in your ghee.

1 lb. or ½ kg. organic, unsalted butter
1 clean, dry glass pint or 500ml jar with a lid
1 cast iron, stainless steel or glass saucepan
1 stainless steel fine mesh strainer

Here's how:

Place butter in a pot and melt over medium-low heat then medium heat to bring to a simmer. It will pop and speak to you. Turn the heat down to medium low and let it simmer uncovered while you stay in the area. No need to touch or stir it. Adjust the heat so that the popping continues but is not splashing out of the pan. Lower is often better here until you get a sense of how your stove and pan respond.

The ghee is ready when the popping stops and it turns amber with residue on the bottom of the pan. Remove it from the heat immediately when the popping stops or it will burn and is not usable. The length of time varies by the amount of butter, the room temperature and humidity, the food the cows ate, the pot used, and the stove. Each experience is unique, but with experience you can get an accurate idea of how long it takes. This recipe uses 1 lb of butter and takes about 15 minutes. Larger amounts of butter will take longer to cook.

Once finished, let the cooked ghee cool a few minutes before straining it through unbleached cheesecloth or a fine mesh strainer into a clean, dry jar. Store it in a cupboard away from the sun.

Note: Be sure to use organic butter, as the quality of a cow's life will greatly affect the quality of your ghee. It's also best to support companies that treat the cows well.

Mahamrityunjaya mantra

Chanting the mahamrityunjaya mantra while making ghee (or any meal) will infuse your ghee with healing vibrations.

Om Triyambakam yajamahe
Sugandhim pushti vardhanam
Urva rukramiva bandhanan
Mrityor mukshiyam amritat

<u>Translation</u>

Give us the opportunity to grow,
prosper, experience, ripen to an old age
then transit in an easy manner
to whatever is next
like a ripe fruit that falls from a tree

Dhal fundamentals

Digestion of legumes

Legumes, including mung beans, are extractive, heavy and drying. Cook them with ghee (or another oil), mineral salt, spices, and water in order to support the digestion and assimilation of the dhal. If using whole mung beans, remember to soak them in advance overnight or for at least 6 hours. Be sure to throw out the soak water before cooking and cook the soaked beans with fresh pure water.

There are many people who feel they can't digest legumes. If the agni — digestive fire — is weak then it can be difficult. By their nature, legumes are more challenging to digest than some other foods. However, this trait is often amplified by improper preparation and consumption.

Here are some examples of common errors in the preparation of legumes that lead to discomfort and compromised digestion:

1.   **Not cooking the legumes enough.** Use a pressure cooker to cut the cooking time down significantly and ensure that your legumes are cooked thoroughly.

2.   **Not spicing the legumes in a way that supports the digestive process.** Remember that spices used in moderation will support agni to do its job.

3.   **Eating too much in one sitting.** If you only eat legumes, or if they make up the majority of your meal, your agni and elimination will be challenged by the heaviness of the beans. For most adults, ⅛ cup of dried beans is sufficient per meal.

4.   **Not including enough augmenting food in the dish.** As we have already learned, balancing the meal with 60% augmenting foods and 40% extractive foods eases digestion and supports elimination.

5.   **Not chewing the legumes thoroughly.** To support agni, all food should be chewed well so that there are no solids swallowed. This allows the food to mix with digestive enzymes in the saliva and prepares the food for the next stage of digestion.

It's easy to avoid these errors — you simply need to integrate the principles and practices outlined in this book into your dhal preparation.

It's worth noting that it's possible to still experience some digestive discomfort or gas even when you prepare and consume a dhal according to Ayurvedic principles. This is because legumes are extractive, so they will move out excess vata in the intestines that accumulates as a result of undigested food lingering there. But if you strengthen your digestion by consistently building your meals according to the 60% augmenting and 40% extractive ratio, then you should soon be able to enjoy legumes comfortably.

Tridoshic preparation

Simplicity is the key to balanced living and cooking. This is why these dhal recipes are primarily tridoshic, which means they are nourishing and will balance all doshas.

Dhal is versatile, and the recipes can be fine-tuned according to the season and to the condition of your agni. By adjusting the consistency of the dhal and the amount and type of spices you use, you can ensure your dish is digestible, balancing and enjoyable year-round.

The type of oil and spices used will render the dish warming or cooling. The amount of each spice will also make a difference in the heating or cooling nature of the dhal. Most digestive spices are warming to support agni, so the overall effect of spicing is typically more warming, however, the degree of warming can be quite distinct.

Warming or cooling?

Whether a more warming or more cooling dhal will bring balance depends on many factors, such as the season, the other dishes in the meal, and the unique needs of the person eating. It's important to support agni as much as possible. Generally speaking, more cooling oils and spices are appropriate in the warm summer, and more warming oils and spices are appropriate in the cold winter.

See the appendix for a list of useful spices.

Thick or thin

The consistency of a dhal impacts its digestibility. By adjusting the amount of water you use, the dhal can be made thicker or thinner.

If you make it thicker it will be more difficult to digest for someone with weaker agni. It's also not best in very hot weather, when agni is naturally weaker. A thin soupy recipe will be appropriate for those with weakened or slow agni or a great place to start for anyone who believes they cannot eat legumes. A person with strong agni who is not constipated may occasionally enjoy a thicker consistency similar to a dumpling. This is a nice choice in the cold winter weather when agni is naturally stronger. A moderate approach to creating the consistency of the dhal will bring the greatest enjoyment of the process and the results, meaning not too much, not too little, avoiding extremes.

Dhal consistency guidelines

Consistency	*Thin, soupy*	*Medium, creamy*	*Thick, dumpling*
Seasonal consideration	*Hot weather*	*Year-round*	*Cold weather*
Condition of agni	*Weak agni, Emphasize if constipated*	*Balanced agni*	*Strong agni, Avoid if constipated*

How to use this book

Globally inspired

The recipes are inspired by my favorite cuisines including Chinese, Indian, Japanese, Middle Eastern (Levante), Mediterranean (including Italian), Mexican, New Zealand and Vietnamese.

The recipes are organized by their cultural influence. At the beginning of each section you will find a complete balance bowl recipe with 4 parts: a grain, a dhal, an augmenting vegetables, and an extractive vegetable. The remaining recipes in each section are all for dhals, but you can take the suggested spice combinations as inspiration for other dishes as well.

Become an alchemist

As you use this book, you will form a relationship with your spices. When you prepare each recipe you will experience a unique, subtle alchemy — a magical process of transformation and creation as ingredients combine with the energy of the moment. You will come to understand how spices used in moderation at the appropriate time will heal. You will experience how food can become your finest medicine.

Choosing the best virya

The virya (warming, cooling, or neutral quality) of the dhal is indicated for each recipe. The degree of the warming and cooling nature is expressed with "+" or "-" after the word warming or cooling for each recipe. Choose your recipe each day based on how you feel inside, the weather outside, and what you have available. Use the principle of opposite qualities bring balance. If you feel hot inside your body then choose a cooling or neutral recipe to support digestion and help to balance dosha. If you feel cool inside your body then choose a warming recipe. Use the more warming recipes on a chilly day, and use the more cooling recipes in warm to hot weather. In hot weather, it's also a good idea to reduce the amount of spicing by ¼ to ½ proportionately to better support agni, which naturally lowers in hot weather to help the body stay cool. The oils used have a virya as well. Sesame and olive oils are warming and coconut oil is cooling. Sunflower and ghee are fairly neutral.

At the end of the book you'll find a handy index of recipes according to virya.

Legume variety

In this recipe book I use two types of mung bean — whole and split — and refer to them as "whole mung beans" and "split mung beans" respectively. They are the same bean, but the split variety has been deshelled and split in half. This makes the split mung bean easier to digest. I have included recipes with whole mung beans in each section to show that they work interchangeably with split mung beans. However, whole mung beans need to soak at least 6 hours in advance and require the longer cooking time explained in the next section: "Five-step cooking method."

Other whole beans such as adzukis or black-eyed peas can be used in these recipes, but they will need to be soaked at least 4-6 hours in advance and require a longer cook time similar to whole mung beans. You might also consider using a legume that grows in your locale although some may be a little more challenging to digest.

Five-step cooking method

The technique for cooking split mung beans is the same no matter what spices or oils you're using. Here are the steps:

1.   Heat the ghee or another oil in a pot over medium heat.

2.   Then, add salt, any fresh root spices like ginger or turmeric, and seed spices as called for in the recipe; simmer until the aroma distinctly comes up to meet you.

3.   Next, add spice powders and fresh herbs and simmer until their aroma is present.

4.   Add split mung beans, stir to coat with ghee and spices and simmer for a few minutes.

5.   Add the amount of water for desired consistency, stir and bring to a boil; reduce to simmer and cover for 25 minutes (stove-top cooking), or 18 minutes (pressure cooker) allowing the pressure to release naturally. Let sit 5 minutes after cooking, stir and serve warm.
Note: If you are cooking whole mung beans (soak at least 6 hours throwing out the soak water) then the cook time is 35 - 40 minutes (stc) or 24 minutes (pc) allowing the pressure cooker to release naturally. Let sit 5 minutes after cooking, stir and serve warm. Cook times may vary depending on your pot or pressure cooker and the temperature in the room.

It's important to cook the spices enough to wake up the prana. This is apparent when the aroma is present. You must cook the spices to wake them up or they are not as effective for supporting agni and the taste of the dhal will be weaker. This is true when cooking other food as well. Once you are comfortable with this simple five-step process, it's easy to make nourishing, digestible and delicious dhals with an infinite number of possibilities.

Measurements and cook times

Measurements in the recipes are for dried legumes. Use approximately ⅛ cup dry measure per person and adjust up or down for the desired thickness and appetites. I provide water measurements, however if you like a thinner consistency then add more water at the beginning of the cooking process. Cook legumes until they mash easily. Too little cooking will leave them difficult to digest.

All of the recipes are for 4 servings and can easily be reduced or expanded proportionately.

The recipes below include cook times for both regular stove top cooking (stc) and cooking using a stove-top pressure cooker (pc). There are also electric pressure cookers available that will take even less time for cooking and can be programmed in advance to turn on at a specific time and turn off when complete! Very handy.

Symbols and abbreviations

Stovetop cooking: stc
Pressure cooker: pc
Virya (feeling of warming/cooling in stomach and small intestines).

- Cooling
- Neutral
- Warming -
- Warming
- Warming +

Intuition and intellect

These recipes are meant to support you to create in the moment with what you have available. You don't need a long list of fancy ingredients. Some of the best traditional dishes from cuisines around the world were created by peasants using simple, seasonal ingredients. In fact, many traditional dishes were developed as a result of scarcity and ingenuity.

If being creative in the moment is a new approach for you then it might feel a little scary. Not to worry, I have given measurements to work with in the recipes. As you become more comfortable, I encourage you to use your intuition in the cooking process as much as possible. Be aware that using your intuition is different from following cravings, which are usually symptoms of imbalanced dosha. An intuitive decision arises not from craving, but from connecting to the intelligence of the food and the state of your body in the moment. To cultivate this connection and sharpen your intuitive abilities in the kitchen, use your hands as often as possible to measure and mix the foods. Rather than relying on measuring cups and spoons, learn to use handfuls for each serving of vegetables and use finger pinches to measure spices. The more your hands contact the food the more connection you cultivate and the more love you can put into it.

Avoid tasting food while cooking. It is disturbing to your own digestion and contributes to a heady, analytical, performance-based approach which does not allow for true creativity and spontaneity in your cooking. If you taste the food as you go, you're more likely to follow your dosha imbalances and this will result in food that will create imbalance in doshas of anyone that consumes it. Consider that the entire process of food preparation and eating is not about satisfying fleeting sensory pleasures, but rather is about providing love and nourishment to the body, mind and soul. No matter what you are preparing to eat, put your feelings of love, peace and joy into the meal for the very best results in terms of taste, digestion, nourishment and enjoyment.

Have fun with these recipes and trust the process. Let it be an adventure. We never know exactly what will happen in life but if we open the mind and heart we get results beyond our imagination. Let your food be an expression of love and delight. Many blessings from Hale Pule.

Chinese recipes

Recipe 1

Complete 60:40 balance bowl recipe

Augmenting 60% of meal: *Rice, carrot*	**Extractive 40% of meal:** *Mung beans, broccoli*

Preparation time: *10 minutes to get the rice and mung beans cooking and chop the veggies then 15 minutes cooking time for the veggies and forming the dumplings (25 minutes total).*	**Serves:** *4*

Prepare the beans and rice first. Halfway through, come back to cook the veggies and serve it all together in a beautiful meal.

Rice & mung dumpling (Warming +)

You'll need:

2	Tbsp ghee
⅓	tsp mineral salt
1	tsp chopped fresh ginger
½	tsp fennel seed
½	tsp star anise seed
¼	tsp cinnamon powder
¼	tsp clove powder
¼	tsp black pepper
½	cup split mung beans
1	cup white rice
	(use a sticky rice if available)
3	cups water

Here's how:

Heat the ghee in a pot over medium heat. Then, add salt, fresh ginger, fennel and star anise seeds; simmer until the aroma comes up to meet you. Next, add cinnamon, clove and black pepper and simmer until the aroma is present. Add split mung beans and rice, stir to coat with ghee and spices and simmer for a few minutes. Add the water, stir and bring to a boil; reduce to simmer and cover for 25 minutes (stc), or 18 minutes (pc) allowing the pressure cooker to release naturally. Let cool until the rice and mung can be formed into dumplings. Serve warm.

Recipe 1 continued

Complete 60:40 balance bowl recipe

Broccoli & carrot clear soup *(Warming)*

You'll need:

3   medium carrots cut in quarters
     thumb length
2   cups chopped broccoli including
     tender stem and florets
1-2 Tbsp ghee
⅓   tsp mineral salt
½   tsp cumin seeds ground
¼   tsp turmeric powder
4   cups water to cover the veggies
Chopped coriander leaves

Here's how:

Heat the oil in a small pan and simmer the salt, and cumin until the aroma is present. Add in the turmeric and simmer briefly. Add the broccoli and carrots and stir to cover with the oil and spices. Add the water, stir, cover and simmer until the veggies can be pierced with a knife. Turn off the heat and add the coriander. Cover and let sit for 5 minutes.

Recipe 2 *(Warming +)*

You'll need:

1-2 Tbsp sesame oil
⅓ tsp mineral salt
2 tsp chopped fresh ginger root
1 finger length piece lemongrass stalk
1 Tbsp chopped kombu
½ tsp ground coriander seeds
2 tsp cumin powder
½ cup split mung beans
1½ cups water

Here's how:

Heat oil in a pot over medium heat. Then, add salt, fresh ginger, lemongrass, kombu and the fenugreek; simmer until the aroma comes up to meet you. Next, add cumin powder and simmer until the aroma is present. Add split mung beans, stir to coat with oil and spices and simmer for a few minutes. Add water, stir and bring to a boil; reduce to simmer and cover for 25 minutes (stc), or 18 minutes (pc), allowing the pressure cooker to release naturally. Let sit 5 minutes after cooking, stir and serve warm.

Recipe 3 *(Warming)*

You'll need:

1-2 Tbsp ghee
⅓ tsp mineral salt
½ tsp cumin seeds
¾ tsp ground black sesame seeds
2-3 tsp chopped hijiki
1 Tbsp coriander powder
½ cup whole mung beans soaked in advance
Water

Here's how:

Heat the ghee in a pot over medium heat. Then, add salt, cumin seeds, black sesame seeds and hijiki; simmer until the aroma comes up to meet you. Next, add coriander powder and simmer until the aroma is present. Add whole mung beans, stir to coat with ghee and spices and simmer for a few minutes. Add water to cover the beans, for desired consistency, stir and bring to a boil; reduce to simmer and cover for 35-40 minutes (stc), or 24 minutes (pc). Allowing the pressure cooker to release naturally then mash the beans into the desired consistency, adding water as needed. Let sit 5 minutes after cooking, stir and serve warm.

Recipe 4 *(Warming)*

You'll need:

1-2	Tbsp ghee
⅓	tsp mineral salt
½	tsp brown mustard seeds
1	Tbsp cumin powder
1	tsp turmeric powder
½	cup split mung beans
2	cups water

Here's how:

Heat the ghee in a pot over medium heat. Then, add salt, brown mustard seeds and simmer until the seeds pop. Next, add cumin and turmeric powders and simmer until the aroma is present. Add split mung beans, stir to coat with ghee and spices and simmer for a few minutes. Add water for the desired consistency, stir and bring to a boil; reduce to simmer and cover for 25 minutes (stc), or 18 minutes (pc), allowing the pressure cooker to release naturally. Let sit 5 minutes after cooking, stir and serve warm.

Recipe 5 *(Warming -)*

You'll need:

2	Tbsp sunflower oil
⅓	tsp mineral salt
2	tsp grated fresh ginger root
2	tsp grated fresh turmeric
¼	tsp ground black pepper
¼	tsp asafoetida (hing)
½	cup split mung beans
1½	cups water

Here's how:

Heat the oil in a pot over medium heat. Then, add salt, fresh ginger and turmeric; simmer until the aroma comes up to meet you. Next, add black pepper and asafoetida and simmer until the aroma is present. Add split mung beans, stir to coat with oil and spices and simmer for a few minutes. Add water, stir and bring to a boil; reduce to simmer and cover for 25 minutes (stc), or 18 minutes (pc), allowing the pressure cooker to release naturally. Let sit 5 minutes after cooking, stir and serve warm.

Recipe 6 *(Warming -)*

You'll need:

1-2	Tbsp ghee
⅓	tsp mineral salt
1	tsp grated ginger root
½	tsp brown mustard seed
1	tsp cumin powder
2	tsp coriander powder
½	cup split mung beans
1½	cups water

Here's how:

Heat the ghee in a pot over medium heat. Then, add salt, ginger root and brown mustard seeds; simmer until the aroma comes up to meet you. Next, add cumin and coriander powder and simmer. Add split mung beans, stir to coat with ghee and spices and simmer for a few minutes. Add water, stir and bring to a boil; reduce to simmer and cover for 25 minutes (stc), or 18 minutes (pc), allowing the pressure cooker to release naturally. Let sit 5 minutes after cooking, stir and serve warm.

Recipe 7 *(Warming +)*

You'll need:

2	Tbsp sesame oil
⅓	tsp mineral salt
1	pinch of chili pepper
½	tsp ginger powder
½	tsp turmeric powder
1	tsp cumin powder
1	tsp coriander powder
½	cup split mung beans
1	Tbsp chopped fresh parsley
4	cups water

Here's how:

Heat oil in a pot over medium heat. Then, add salt, chili, ginger, turmeric, cumin and coriander powders; simmer until the aroma comes up to meet you. Add split mung beans, stir to coat with oil and spices and simmer for a few minutes. Add the water for a soup consistency, stir and bring to a boil; reduce to simmer and cover for 25 minutes (stc), or 18 minutes (pc), allowing the pressure cooker to release naturally. Add the parsley and let sit 5 minutes after cooking, stir and serve warm.

Indian recipes

Recipe 8
Complete 60:40 balance bowl recipe

Augmenting 60% of meal: Carrot, brown and white jasmine rice	**Extractive 40% of meal:** Kale, split mung
Preparation time: 10 minutes to get rice and mung beans cooking and chop the veggies then 10-15 minutes cooking time for veggies. Prepare the beans and rice first (25 minutes total).	**Serves:** 4

Halfway through cooking come back to cook the veggies and serve it all together in a beautiful meal.

Mung beans *(Warming +)*

You'll need:

1-2   Tbsp ghee
⅓   tsp mineral salt
½   tsp ginger root
¾   tsp mustard seeds
1   tsp cumin powder
1   tsp coriander powder
4-6   curry leaves
½   tsp black pepper
½   cup split mung beans
1½   cups water

Here's how:

Heat the ghee in a pot over medium heat. Then, add salt, ginger root and brown mustard seeds; simmer until the aroma comes up to meet you. Next, add cumin and coriander powders, black pepper and curry leaves and simmer until the aroma is present. Add split mung beans, stir to coat with ghee and spices and simmer for a few minutes. Add water, stir and bring to a boil; reduce to simmer and cover for 25 minutes (stc), or 18 minutes (pc), allowing the pressure cooker to release naturally. Let sit 5 minutes after cooking, stir and serve warm.

Rice *(Neutral)*

You'll need:

½   cup brown jasmine rice
½   cup white jasmine rice
2   tsp ghee
⅓   tsp mineral salt
½   tsp coriander powder
2   cups water

Here's how:

Heat the oil in a small pot and simmer the salt and coriander powder until the aroma is present. Add the rice and stir, simmering for 1-2 minutes. Add the water, stir, cover and simmer for 35 minutes until the water is absorbed and the brown rice is plump and softish. Turn off the heat and let sit 5 minutes before serving. This can also be cooked in a rice cooker, pressure cooker or clay pot with appropriate time adjustments.

<u>Recipe 8 continued</u>
Complete 60:40 balance bowl recipe

Carrots *(Warming)*

You'll need:

2	medium carrots cut in quarters thumb length
1	Tbsp ghee
⅓	tsp mineral salt
½	tsp cumin seeds ground
½	tsp fennel seeds ground
¼	tsp turmeric powder

Water to ¼ height of veggie
Chopped coriander leaves

Here's how:

Heat the oil in a small pan and simmer the salt, cumin, and fennel until the aroma is present. Add in the turmeric and simmer briefly. Add the carrots and stir to cover with the oil and spices. Add the water, stir, cover and simmer until tender and can be pierced with a knife. Turn off the heat and add the coriander. Cover and let sit for 5 minutes.

Kale *(Warming +)*

You'll need:

4	cups fresh chopped kale (or small leaves)
2	Tbsp sesame oil
¾	tsp mineral salt
1	tsp ground black or white sesame seeds
⅛	tsp ajwain seeds
3	Tbsp chopped skinned almonds
½	lime for juice

Water to ¼ height of veggie

Here's how:

Heat the oil in a small pan and simmer the salt, sesame, ajwain, and almonds until the aroma is present. Add the kale and stir to cover with the oil and spices. Add water, stir, cover and simmer until tender. Turn off the heat and add a small squeeze of lime. Cover and let sit for 5 minutes.

Recipe 9 *(Warming -)*

You'll need:

1-2	Tbsp ghee
⅓	tsp mineral salt
2	tsp fresh chopped ginger root
⅓	tsp asafoetida (hing)
1	Tbsp coriander powder
4	curry leaves
½	cup whole mung beans soaked in advance
Water	

Here's how:

Heat the ghee in a pot over medium heat. Then, add salt and ginger root and simmer until the aroma comes up to meet you. Next, add asafoetida, coriander powder and curry leaves and simmer until the aroma is present. Add whole mung beans, stir to coat with ghee and spices and simmer for a few minutes. Add water to cover the beans, stir and bring to a boil; reduce to simmer and cover for 35-40 minutes (stc), or 24 minutes (pc), allowing the pressure cooker to release naturally. Let sit 5 minutes after cooking, stir and serve warm.

Recipe 10 *(Warming +)*

You'll need:

1-2	Tbsp ghee
⅓	tsp mineral salt
1	tsp grated fresh ginger
1	tiny pinch fresh chili
¾	tsp brown mustard seeds
¼	tsp ajwain seeds (Indian celery seed)
1	tsp turmeric powder
2	tsp cumin powder
2	tsp coriander powder
½	cup split mung beans
1½	cups water

Here's how:

Heat the ghee in a pot over medium heat. Then, add salt, ginger, chili, brown mustard seeds and ajwain seeds; simmer until the aroma comes up to meet you. Next, add turmeric, cumin and coriander powders and simmer until the aroma is present. Add split mung beans, stir to coat with ghee and spices and simmer for a few minutes. Add water, stir and bring to a boil; reduce to simmer and cover for 25-30 minutes (stc), or 18 minutes (pc), allowing the pressure cooker to release naturally. Let sit 5 minutes after cooking, stir and serve warm.

Recipe 11 *(Warming +)*

You'll need:

1-2	Tbsp ghee
⅓	tsp mineral salt
½	tsp fennel seed
½	tsp cumin seed
¼	tsp asafoetida
6	curry leaves
¼	cup chopped parsley
½	cup split mung beans
1½	cups water

Here's how:

Heat the ghee in a pot over medium heat. Then, add salt, fennel and cumin seeds; simmer until the aroma comes up to meet you. Next, add asafoetida and curry leaves and simmer until the aroma is present. Add split mung beans, stir to coat with ghee and spices and simmer for a few minutes. Add water, stir and bring to a boil; reduce to simmer and cover for 25 minutes (stc), or 18 minutes (pc), allowing the pressure cooker to release naturally. Stir in the chopped parsley and let sit 5 minutes after cooking, stir and serve warm.

Recipe 12 *(Warming)*

You'll need:

1-2	Tbsp ghee
⅓	tsp mineral salt
1	tsp fresh chopped ginger root
1	tsp fresh chopped turmeric
1	tsp fenugreek powder
½	cup split mung beans
1½	cups tea made from equal amounts of cumin, coriander and fennel seeds (soaked overnight and brought to a boil as a digestive tea)

Pinch of cinnamon powder

Here's how:

Heat the ghee in a pot over medium heat. Then, add salt, ginger and turmeric roots and simmer until the aroma comes up to meet you. Next, add fenugreek and cinnamon powders and simmer until the aroma is present. Add split mung beans, stir to coat with ghee and spices and simmer for a few minutes. Add tea, stir and bring to a boil; reduce to simmer and cover for 25 minutes (stc), or 18 minutes (pc), allowing the pressure cooker to release naturally. Let sit 5 minutes after cooking, stir and serve warm.

Recipe 13 *(Warming)*

You'll need:

1-2	Tbsp ghee
⅓	tsp mineral salt
½	tsp black cumin seed
½	tsp fenugreek seeds
1	tsp turmeric powder
½	cup whole mung beans soaked in advance
Water	

Here's how:

Heat the ghee in a pot over medium heat. Then, add salt, black cumin seeds and fenugreek seeds; simmer until the aroma comes up to meet you. Next, add turmeric powder and simmer until the aroma is present. Add whole mung beans, stir to coat with ghee and spices and simmer for a few minutes. Add water to cover, stir and bring to a boil; reduce to simmer and cover for 35 - 40 minutes (stc), or 24 minutes (pc), allowing the pressure cooker to release naturally. Let sit 5 minutes after cooking, stir and serve warm.

Recipe 14 *(Warming +)*

You'll need:

2	Tbsp sesame oil
½	tsp mineral salt
½	tsp black cumin seeds
½	tsp fenugreek powder
¼	tsp ginger powder
½	cup brown lentils soaked in advance
4	cups water

Here's how:

Heat the oil in a pot over medium heat. Then, add salt and cumin seeds; simmer until the aroma comes up to meet you. Next, add fenugreek and ginger powders and simmer until the aroma is present. Add brown lentils, stir to coat with oil and spices and simmer for a few minutes. Add water for a soup consistency, stir and bring to a boil; reduce to simmer and cover for 30 minutes (stc), or 22 minutes (pc), allowing the pressure cooker to release naturally. Let sit 5 minutes after cooking, stir and serve warm.

Recipe 15 *(Warming)*

You'll need:

1-2	Tbsp ghee
½	tsp salt
2	tsp fresh chopped ginger
1	tsp fresh chopped turmeric
½	tsp black cumin seeds
½	tsp asafoetida
½	cup split mung beans
2	cups water

Here's how:

Heat the ghee in a pot over medium heat. Then, add salt, ginger and turmeric root and black cumin seeds; simmer until the aroma comes up to meet you. Next, add asafoetida powder and simmer until the aroma is present. Add split mung beans, stir to coat with ghee and spices and simmer for a few minutes. Add water, stir and bring to a boil; reduce to simmer and cover for 25 minutes (stc), or 18 minutes (pc), allowing the pressure cooker to release naturally. Let sit 5 minutes after cooking, stir and serve warm.

Recipe 16 *(Warming +)*

You'll need:

1-2	Tbsp ghee
⅓	tsp mineral salt
¼	tsp fenugreek seeds
½	tsp ginger powder
1	tsp ground coriander
2	bay leaves
½	cup split mung beans
1½	cups water

Here's how:

Heat the ghee in a pot over medium heat. Then, add salt, fenugreek seeds and simmer until the aroma comes up to meet you. Next, add ginger powder, coriander powder and bay leaves and simmer until the aroma is present. Add split mung beans, stir to coat with ghee and spices and simmer for a few minutes. Add water, stir and bring to a boil; reduce to simmer and cover for 25 minutes (stc), or 18 minutes (pc), allowing the pressure cooker to release naturally. Let sit 5 minutes after cooking, stir and serve warm.

Recipe 17 (Warming +)

You'll need:

1-2	Tbsp ghee
⅓	tsp mineral salt
½	tsp black sesame seeds
½	tsp fenugreek seeds
1	tsp cumin powder
¼	tsp fenugreek powder
½	tsp turmeric powder
½	cup whole mung beans soaked in advance
Water	

Here's how:

Heat the ghee in a pot over medium heat. Then, add salt, black sesame seeds and fenugreek seeds; simmer until the aroma comes up to meet you. Next, add cumin, fenugreek and turmeric powder and simmer until the aroma is present. Add whole mung beans, stir to coat with ghee and spices and simmer for a few minutes. Add water to cover the beans, stir and bring to a boil; reduce to simmer and cover for 35-40 minutes (stc), or 24 minutes (pc), allowing the pressure cooker to release naturally. Let sit 5 minutes after cooking, stir and serve warm.

Recipe 18 (Warming)

You'll need:

1-2	Tbsp ghee
⅓	tsp mineral salt
1	tsp fresh turmeric root
1	tsp cumin seed
1	tsp fennel powder
¼	tsp asafoetida
½	cup split mung beans
2	cups water

Here's how:

Heat the ghee in a pot over medium heat. Then, add salt, turmeric and cumin seeds; simmer until the aroma comes up to meet you. Next, add fennel and asafoetida and simmer until the aroma is present. Add split mung beans, stir to coat with ghee and spices and simmer for a few minutes. Add water, stir and bring to a boil; reduce to simmer and cover for 25 minutes (stc), or 18 minutes (pc), allowing the pressure cooker to release naturally. Let sit 5 minutes after cooking, stir and serve warm.

Recipe 19 (Warming)

You'll need:

1-2	Tbsp ghee
⅓	tsp mineral salt
1	tsp fresh chopped ginger
1	tsp fresh chopped turmeric
½	tsp black sesame seeds
½	tsp fenugreek powder
½	cup split mung beans
1½	cups water

Here's how:

Heat the ghee in a pot over medium heat. Then, add salt, chopped ginger and turmeric and black sesame seeds; simmer until the aroma comes up to meet you. Next, add fenugreek powder and simmer until the aroma is present. Add split mung beans, stir to coat with ghee and spices and simmer for a few minutes. Add water, stir and bring to a boil; reduce to simmer and cover for 25 minutes (stc), or 18 minutes (pc), allowing the pressure cooker to release naturally. Let sit 5 minutes after cooking, stir and serve warm.

Recipe 20 (Warming +)

You'll need:

1½	Tbsp ghee
⅓	tsp mineral salt
1	tsp cumin seed
1	tsp fennel seed
½	tsp asafoetida powder
½	tsp tulsi basil leaves
½	cup split mung beans
4	cups water

Here's how:

Heat the ghee in a pot over medium heat. Then, add salt, cumin and fennel seeds; simmer until the aroma comes up to meet you. Next, add asafoetida and basil and simmer until the aroma is present. Add split mung beans, stir to coat with ghee and spices and simmer for a few minutes. Add water, stir and bring to a boil; reduce to simmer and cover for 25 minutes (stc), or 18 minutes (pc), allowing the pressure cooker to release naturally. Let sit 5 minutes after cooking, stir and serve warm.

Recipe 21 *(Warming +)*

You'll need:

1-2	Tbsp ghee
⅓	tsp mineral salt
¾	tsp cumin seeds
¼	tsp fenugreek seeds
1	tsp turmeric powder
2-4	curry leaves
½	cup split mung beans
2	cups water

Here's how:

Heat the ghee in a pot over medium heat. Then, add salt, cumin and fenugreek seeds; simmer until the aroma comes up to meet you. Next, add turmeric and curry leaves and simmer until the aroma is present. Add split mung beans, stir to coat with ghee and spices and simmer for a few minutes. Add water, stir and bring to a boil; reduce to simmer and cover for 25 minutes (stc), or 18 minutes (pc), allowing the pressure cooker to release naturally. Let sit 5 minutes after cooking, stir and serve warm.

Recipe 22 *(Neutral)*

You'll need:

1	Tbsp sunflower oil
2	tsp ghee
⅓	tsp mineral salt
2	tsp chopped fresh ginger root
½	tsp fennel seeds
¼	tsp brown mustard seeds
¼	tsp asafoetida
½	cup split mung beans
1½	cup water

Here's how:

Heat the ghee and sunflower oil in a pot over medium heat. Then, add salt, ginger root, fennel and brown mustard seeds; simmer until the aroma comes up to meet you. Next, add asafoetida and simmer until the aroma is present. Add split mung beans, stir to coat with ghee and spices and simmer for a few minutes. Add water, stir and bring to a boil; reduce to simmer and cover for 25 minutes (stc), or 18 minutes (pc), allowing the pressure cooker to release naturally. Let sit 5 minutes after cooking, stir and serve warm.

Recipe 23 *(Warming)*

You'll need:

1-2 Tbsp ghee
⅓ tsp mineral salt
½ tsp grated fresh ginger root
½ tsp brown mustard seeds
¼ tsp fennel seeds
1 Tbsp cumin powder
½ cup split mung beans
1½ cups water
Pinch of cinnamon powder

Here's how:

Heat the ghee in a pot over medium heat. Then, add salt, ginger root, brown mustard and fennel seeds; simmer until the aroma comes up to meet you. Next, add cumin and cinnamon powder and simmer until the aroma is present. Add split mung beans, stir to coat with ghee and spices and simmer for a few minutes. Add water, stir and bring to a boil; reduce to simmer and cover for 25 minutes (stc), or 18 minutes (pc), allowing the pressure cooker to release naturally. Let sit 5 minutes after cooking, stir and serve warm.

Recipe 24 *(Neutral)*

You'll need:

1-2 Tbsp ghee
⅓ tsp mineral salt
½ tsp cardamom seeds
2 tsp fennel powder
½ tsp asafoetida
½ cup whole mung beans
soaked in advance
Pinch of ground black pepper
Water

Here's how:

Heat the ghee in a pot over medium heat. Then, add salt, cardamom seeds and black pepper; simmer until the aroma comes up to meet you. Next, add fennel and asafoetida powder and simmer until the aroma is present. Add whole mung beans, stir to coat with ghee and spices and simmer for a few minutes. Add water to cover the beans, stir and bring to a boil; reduce to simmer and cover for 35 - 40 minutes (stc), or 24 minutes (pc), allowing the pressure cooker to release naturally. Let sit 5 minutes after cooking, stir and serve warm.

Recipe 25 *(Warming +)*

You'll need:

1-2	Tbsp ghee
⅓	tsp mineral salt
½	tsp fresh grated ginger root
½	tsp fresh grated turmeric root
1	inch of cinnamon bark stick
¼	tsp ajwain seeds
½	tsp fenugreek powder
½	tsp fennel powder
¼	tsp asafoetida
½	cup whole mung beans soaked in advance

Pinch of clove powder
Water

Here's how:

Heat the ghee in a pot over medium heat. Then, add salt, ginger and turmeric root, cinnamon stick and ajwain seeds; simmer until the aroma comes up to meet you. Next, add fenugreek, fennel, asafoetida and clove powder and simmer until the aroma is present. Add whole mung beans, stir to coat with ghee and spices and simmer for a few minutes. Add water, stir and bring to a boil; reduce to simmer and cover for 35-40 minutes (stc), or 24 minutes (pc), allowing the pressure cooker to release naturally. Let sit 5 minutes after cooking, stir and serve warm.

Recipe 26 *(Neutral)*

You'll need:

1	Tbsp ghee
1	Tbsp coconut oil
⅓	tsp mineral salt
½	tsp cardamom seeds
½	tsp brown mustard seeds
1	Tbsp coriander powder
2-4	curry leaves
½	cup split mung beans
1½	cups water

Pinch of ground black pepper

Here's how:

Heat the ghee and coconut oil in a pot over medium heat. Then, add salt, cardamom, mustard seeds and ground black pepper; simmer until the aroma comes up to meet you. Next, add coriander powder and curry leaves and simmer until the aroma is present. Add split mung beans, stir to coat with oil and spices and simmer for a few minutes. Add water, stir and bring to a boil; reduce to simmer and cover for 25 minutes (stc), or 18 minutes (pc), allowing the pressure cooker to release naturally. Let sit 5 minutes after cooking, stir and serve warm.

Recipe 27 (Cooling)

You'll need:

2	Tbsp coconut oil
⅓	tsp mineral salt
2	tsp coriander powder
½	tsp turmeric powder
½	cup chopped fresh mint
½	cup split mung beans
2	cups water

Here's how:

Heat the oil in a pot over medium heat. Then, add salt, coriander and turmeric powders; simmer until the aroma comes up to meet you. Add split mung beans, stir to coat with oil and spices and simmer for a few minutes. Add water, stir and bring to a boil; reduce to simmer and cover for 25 minutes (stc), or 18 minutes (pc), allowing the pressure cooker to release naturally. Add the mint and stir. Let sit 5 minutes after cooking, stir and serve warm.

Recipe 28 (Cooling)

You'll need:

1½	Tbsp ghee
⅓	tsp mineral salt
¾	tsp fennel seeds
2	tsp dried mint leaves
¼	tsp asafoetida
½	cup split mung beans
1½	cups water

Here's how:

Heat the ghee in a pot over medium heat. Then, add salt and fennel seeds; simmer until the aroma comes up to meet you. Next, add mint leaves and asafoetida powder and simmer until the aroma is present. Add split mung beans, stir to coat with ghee and spices and simmer for a few minutes. Add water, stir and bring to a boil; reduce to simmer and cover for 25 minutes (stc), or 18 minutes (pc), allowing the pressure cooker to release naturally. Let sit 5 minutes after cooking, stir and serve warm.

Recipe 29 *(Warming +)*

You'll need:

1-2	Tbsp ghee
⅓	tsp mineral salt
2	tsp chopped ginger
¾	tsp cumin powder
¾	tsp coriander powder
¾	tsp turmeric powder
½	tsp cardamom powder
½	tsp asafoetida powder
½	cup split mung beans
1½	cups water

Here's how:

Heat the ghee in a pot over medium heat. Then, add salt and ginger root; simmer until the aroma comes up to meet you. Next, add cumin, coriander, turmeric, cardamom and asafoetida powders and simmer until the aroma is present. Add split mung, stir to coat with ghee and spices and simmer for a few minutes. Add water, stir and bring to a boil; reduce to simmer and cover for 25 minutes (stc), or 18 minutes (pc), allowing the pressure cooker to release naturally. Let sit 5 minutes after cooking, stir and serve warm.

Japanese recipes

Recipe 30
Complete 60:40 balance bowl recipe

Augmenting 60% of meal: *Rice, zucchini*	***Extractive 40% of meal:*** *Mung beans, spinach*
Preparation time: *10 minutes to get rice and mung beans cooking and chop the veggies then 10-15 minutes cooking time for veggies. Prepare the beans and rice first (25 minutes total).*	***Serves:*** *4*

Halfway through come back to cook the veggies and serve it all together in a beautiful meal.

Mung beans *(Warming)*

You'll need:

2	Tbsp sesame oil
⅓	tsp mineral salt
1	tsp fresh grated ginger root
1	Tbsp coriander powder
½	tsp asafoetida powder
1	Tbsp flaked or thumb length of kombu
½	cup whole mung beans soaked in advance
Water	

Here's how:

Heat the oil in a pot over medium heat. Then, add salt and ginger root; simmer until the aroma comes up to meet you. Next, add coriander and asafoetida powders and kombu; simmer until the aroma is present. Add whole mung beans, stir to coat with oil and spices and simmer for a few minutes. Add water to cover the beans, stir and bring to a boil; reduce to simmer and cover for 35 -40 minutes (stc), or 24 minutes (pc), allowing the pressure cooker to release naturally. Let sit 5 minutes after cooking, stir and serve warm.

Rice *(Neutral)*

You'll need:

½	cup brown sushi rice
½	cup white sushi rice
1	tsp ghee
⅓	tsp mineral salt
2	cups water

Here's how:

Heat the oil and salt in a small pot and add the rice and stir, simmering for 1-2 minutes. Add the water, stir, cover and simmer for 35 minutes until the water is absorbed and the brown rice is plump and softish. Turn off the heat and let sit 5 minutes before serving. This can also be cooked in a rice cooker, pressure cooker or clay pot with appropriate time adjustments.

<u>Recipe 30 continued</u>
Complete 60:40 balance bowl recipe

Zucchini *(Warming -)*

You'll need:

2	medium zucchini cut in quarters thumb length
1	Tbsp ghee
⅓	tsp mineral salt
½	tsp cumin seeds ground
½	tsp fennel seeds ground
¼	tsp turmeric powder

Water to ¼ height of veggie
Chopped coriander leaves

Here's how:

Heat the oil in a small pan and simmer the salt, cumin, and fennel until the aroma is present. Add in the turmeric and simmer briefly. Add the zucchini and stir to cover with the oil and spices. Add the water, stir, cover and simmer until tender and can be pierced with a knife. Turn off the heat and add the coriander. Cover and let sit for 5 minutes.

Spinach *(Warming)*

You'll need:

4	cups fresh chopped spinach (or baby leaves)
¼	cup grated burdock root (optional)
2	Tbsp sesame oil
¾	tsp mineral salt
1	tsp ground black or white sesame seeds
⅛	tsp sancho
¼	lime or lemon

Water to ¼ height of veggie

Here's how:

Heat the oil in a small pan and simmer the salt, sesame seeds, and sancho until the aroma is present. Add the spinach and stir to cover with the oil and spices. Add water, stir, cover and simmer until tender. Turn off the heat and add a small squeeze of lime or lemon. Cover and let sit for 5 minutes.

Recipe 31 *(Warming)*

You'll need:

1-2	Tbsp ghee
½	tsp salt
¼	tsp ground black pepper
½	tsp fenugreek powder
2	tsp nori flakes
½	cup split peas soaked in advance
½	cup split mung beans
2½	cups water

Here's how:

Heat the ghee in a pot over medium heat. Then, add salt and ground black pepper; simmer until the aroma comes up to meet you. Next, add fenugreek powder and nori and simmer until the aroma is present. Add split peas and split mung beans, stir to coat with ghee and spices and simmer for a few minutes. Add water, stir and bring to a boil; reduce to simmer and cover for 25 minutes (stc), or 18 minutes (pc), allowing the pressure cooker to release naturally. Let sit 5 minutes after cooking, stir and serve warm.

Recipe 32 *(Neutral)*

You'll need:

2	Tbsp sunflower oil
⅓	tsp mineral salt
1	tsp fresh chopped ginger
1	strip chopped wakame
½	cup split mung beans
1½	cups water
Pinch of white pepper	

Here's how:

Heat the oil in a pot over medium heat. Then, add salt, ginger root, wakame and pepper; simmer until the aroma comes up to meet you. Add split mung beans, stir to coat with oil and spices and simmer for a few minutes. Add water, stir and bring to a boil; reduce to simmer and cover for 25 minutes (stc), or 18 minutes (pc), allowing the pressure cooker to release naturally. Let sit 5 minutes after cooking, stir and serve warm.

Recipe 33 *(Warming)*

You'll need:

1-2	Tbsp ghee
⅓	tsp mineral salt
1	tsp fresh chopped ginger root
½	tsp cumin seeds
1	tsp chopped kombu
1	tsp coriander powder
1	tsp turmeric powder
½	cup whole mung beans soaked in advance
	Water

Here's how:

Heat the ghee in a pot over medium heat. Then, add salt, ginger root, cumin seeds and kombu; simmer until the aroma comes up to meet you. Next, add coriander and turmeric powders and simmer until the aroma is present. Add whole mung beans, stir to coat with ghee and spices and simmer for a few minutes. Add water to cover the beans, stir and bring to a boil; reduce to simmer and cover for 35-40 minutes (stc), or 24 minutes (pc), allowing the pressure cooker to release naturally. Let sit 5 minutes after cooking, stir and serve warm.

Recipe 34 *(Warming)*

You'll need:

1	Tbsp sesame oil
1	Tbsp ghee
⅓	tsp mineral salt
1	tsp fresh turmeric
½	tsp ground coriander seeds
½	tsp asafoetida
2	tsp flaked nori
½	cup split mung beans
1½	cups water

Here's how:

Heat the oil and ghee in a pot over medium heat. Then, add salt, turmeric root and coriander seeds; simmer until the aroma comes up to meet you. Next, add asafoetida and nori and simmer until the aroma is present. Add split mung beans, stir to coat with oil and spices and simmer for a few minutes. Add water, stir and bring to a boil; reduce to simmer and cover for 25 minutes (stc), or 18 minutes (pc), allowing the pressure cooker to release naturally. Let sit 5 minutes after cooking, stir and serve warm.

Recipe 35 *(Neutral)*

You'll need:

1½	Tbsp sunflower oil
⅓	tsp mineral salt
1	tsp cumin powder
1	tsp coriander powder
1	tsp fennel powder
1	Tbsp fresh chopped shiso leaf
1	Tbsp hijiki
½	cup whole mung beans soaked in advance

Water

Here's how:

Heat the oil in a pot over medium heat. Then, add salt, cumin, coriander, fennel powders and shiso; simmer until the aroma comes up to meet you. Add whole mung beans, stir to coat with oil and spices and simmer for a few minutes. Add water to cover the beans completely, stir and bring to a boil; reduce to simmer and cover for 35-40 minutes (stc), or 24 minutes (pc), allowing the pressure cooker to release naturally. Let sit 5 minutes after cooking, stir and serve warm.

Recipe 36 *(Warming +)*

You'll need:

1-2	Tbsp ghee
⅓	tsp mineral salt
1	tsp fresh chopped ginger root
¼	tsp fenugreek seeds
1	tsp sea weed
¼	tsp wasabi paste
½	cup split mung beans
1½	cups water

Here's how:

Heat the ghee in a pot over medium heat. Then, add salt, ginger root and fenugreek seeds; simmer until the aroma comes up to meet you. Next, add seaweed and wasabi and simmer lightly. Add split mung beans, stir to coat with ghee and spices and simmer for a few minutes. Add water, stir and bring to a boil; reduce to simmer and cover for 25 minutes (stc), or 18 minutes (pc), allowing the pressure cooker to release naturally. Let sit 5 minutes after cooking, stir and serve warm.

Recipe 37 *(Warming)*

You'll need:

1	Tbsp ghee
1	Tbsp sunflower oil
⅓	tsp mineral salt
1	tsp fresh grated ginger
1	tsp fresh grated turmeric
½	tsp ume paste
½	cup split mung beans
2	cups water

Large pinch of arame

Here's how:

Heat the ghee in a pot over medium heat. Then, add salt, ginger and turmeric root and arame; simmer until the aroma comes up to meet you. Add split mung, stir to coat with ghee and spices and simmer for a few minutes. Add water, stir and bring to a boil; reduce to simmer and cover for 25 minutes (stc), or 18 minutes (pc), allowing the pressure cooker to release naturally. Open and stir in ume paste. Let sit 5 minutes after cooking, stir and serve warm.

Recipe 38 *(Neutral)*

You'll need:

1-2	Tbsp ghee
⅓	tsp mineral salt
1	tsp fresh chopped ginger root
2	tsp chopped fresh basil
1	tsp dried mint leaves
1	tsp dried shiso leaves
½	cup split mung beans
1½	cups water

Here's how:

Heat the ghee in a pot over medium heat. Then, add salt and ginger root and simmer until the aroma comes up to meet you. Next, add basil, mint and shiso leaves and simmer until the aroma is present. Add split mung, stir to coat with ghee and spices and simmer for a few minutes. Add water, stir and bring to a boil; reduce to simmer and cover for 25 minutes (stc), or 18 minutes (pc), allowing the pressure cooker to release naturally. Let sit 5 minutes after cooking, stir and serve warm.

Recipe 39 *(Warming)*

You'll need:

1-2	Tbsp ghee
⅓	tsp mineral salt
1	tsp fresh chopped ginger
½	tsp ground sesame seeds
½	tsp turmeric powder
2	tsp coriander powder
1	Tbsp chopped kombu
½	cup split mung beans
3	cups water

Here's how:

Heat the ghee in a pot over medium heat. Then, add salt, ginger root and sesame seeds; simmer until the aroma comes up to meet you. Next, add turmeric and coriander powders and kombu; simmer until the aroma is present. Add split mung beans, stir to coat with ghee and spices and simmer for a few minutes. Add water for a soup consistency, stir and bring to a boil; reduce to simmer and cover for 25 minutes (stc), or 18 minutes (pc), allowing the pressure cooker to release naturally. Let sit 5 minutes after cooking, stir and serve warm.

Recipe 40 *(Warming)*

You'll need:

1-2	Tbsp ghee
⅓	tsp mineral salt
1	tsp fresh grated ginger
½	tsp brown mustard seeds
½	tsp turmeric powder
1	tsp chopped dried curry leaves
½	cup split mung beans
1½	cups water

Here's how:

Heat the ghee in a pot over medium heat. Then, add salt, ginger root and brown mustard seeds; simmer until the aroma comes up to meet you. Next, add turmeric powder and curry leaves and simmer until the aroma is present. Add split mung beans, stir to coat with ghee and spices and simmer for a few minutes. Add water, stir and bring to a boil; reduce to simmer and cover for 25 minutes (stc), or 18 minutes (pc), allowing the pressure cooker to release naturally. Let sit 5 minutes after cooking, stir and serve warm.

Recipe 41 *(Warming +)*

You'll need:

2	Tbsp sesame oil
⅓	tsp mineral salt
½	tsp black cumin seeds
1	tsp sesame seeds
¼	tsp ground black pepper
2	tsp chopped kombu
½	cup split mung beans
1½	cups water

Here's how:

Heat the oil in a pot over medium heat. Then, add salt, cumin and sesame seeds; simmer until the aroma comes up to meet you. Next, add black pepper and simmer until the aroma is present. Add split mung, stir to coat with oil and spices and simmer for a few minutes. Add water, stir and bring to a boil; reduce to simmer and cover for 25 minutes (stc), or 18 minutes (pc), allowing the pressure cooker to release naturally. Let sit 5 minutes after cooking, stir and serve warm.

Recipe 42 *(Warming)*

You'll need:

1-2	Tbsp ghee
⅓	tsp mineral salt
1	Tbsp cumin powder
2	tsp coriander powder
½	tsp fenugreek powder
½	cup split mung beans
1½	cups water

Here's how:

Heat the ghee in a pot over medium heat. Then, add salt, cumin, coriander and fenugreek powders; simmer until the aroma comes up to meet you. Add split mung beans, stir to coat with ghee and spices and simmer for a few minutes. Add water, stir and bring to a boil; reduce to simmer and cover for 25 minutes (stc), or 18 minutes (pc), allowing the pressure cooker to release naturally. Let sit 5 minutes after cooking, stir and serve warm.

Middle Eastern recipes

Recipe 43

Complete 60:40 balance bowl recipe

Augmenting 60% of meal: *Rice and beetroot*	***Extractive 40% of meal:*** *Mung beans, cabbage and celery*
Preparation time: *10 minutes to get rice and mung beans cooking and chop the veggies then 10-15 minutes cooking time for veggies.*	***Serves:*** *4*
Prepare the beans and rice first. Halfway through come back to cook the veggies and serve it all together in a beautiful meal.	

Mung beans (Neutral)

You'll need:

1-2	Tbsp ghee
1	tsp chopped fresh ginger
1	Tbsp chopped fresh mint
2	Tbsp tahini
⅓	tsp mineral salt
½	tsp turmeric powder
½	tsp lime or lemon juice
½	cup whole mung beans soaked in advance

Water to cover the beans

Here's how:

Heat the ghee in a pot over medium heat. Then, add salt and ginger. Simmer until the aroma comes up to meet you. Add the turmeric powder and mint; simmer until the aroma is present. Add whole mung beans, stir to coat with ghee and spices and simmer for a few minutes. Add water, stir and bring to a boil; reduce to simmer and cover for 35-40 minutes (stc), or 24 minutes (pc), allowing the pressure cooker to release naturally. To make a hummus let the beans cool and then blend them in their own liquid with 2 Tbsp tahini and ½ tsp lime or lemon juice. Serve warm or at room temperature.

Rice (Neutral)

You'll need:

1	cup high quality brown or white rice
1	Tbsp ghee
⅓	tsp mineral salt
2	tsp chopped fresh or dried dill
2	cups water

Here's how:

Heat the oil in a small pot and simmer the salt and coriander powder until the aroma is present. Add the rice and stir, simmering for 1-2 minutes. Add the water, stir, cover and simmer for 25 minutes until the water is ¾ absorbed. Add the dill and finish cooking until the brown rice is plump and softish. Turn off the heat and let sit 5 minutes before serving. This can also be cooked in a rice cooker, pressure cooker or clay pot with appropriate time adjustments.

Beetroot *(Warming -)*

You'll need:

2	medium beetroots chopped to bite size
1-2	Tbsp ghee
⅓	tsp mineral salt
½	tsp fennel seeds ground
¼	tsp turmeric powder

Water to ¼ height of veggie

Here's how:

Heat the oil in a small pan and simmer the salt, and fennel until the aroma is present. Add in the turmeric and simmer briefly. Add the beetroot and stir to cover with the oil and spices. Add the water, stir, cover and simmer until tender and can be pierced with a knife. Turn off the heat and let sit for 5 minutes.

Cabbage and Celery *(Warming -)*

You'll need:

3	cups fresh chopped cabbage
1	cup fresh chopped celery
2	Tbsp olive oil
¾	tsp mineral salt
1	tsp ground black or white sesame seeds
¼	tsp sumac or hibiscus
3	Tbsp chopped skinned almonds
¼	lime or lemon

Water to ¼ height of veggie

Here's how:

Heat the oil in a small pan and simmer the salt, sesame seeds, sumac, and almonds until the aroma is present. Add the cabbage and celery and stir to cover with the oil and spices. Add water, stir, cover and simmer until tender. Turn off the heat and add a small squeeze of lime. Cover and let sit for 5 minutes.

Recipe 44 *(Warming)*

You'll need:

1	Tbsp olive oil
1	Tbsp ghee
⅓	tsp mineral salt
¼	tsp ground black pepper
1	tsp cumin powder
¼	tsp cinnamon powder
¼	tsp lemon juice
½	cup split mung beans
1½	cups water
Pinch of nutmeg	

Here's how:

Heat the oil in a pot over medium heat. Then, add salt and black pepper; simmer until the aroma comes up to meet you. Next, add cumin, cinnamon and nutmeg powders and lemon; simmer until the aroma is present. Add split mung beans, stir to coat with oil and spices and simmer for a few minutes. Add water, stir and bring to a boil; reduce to simmer and cover for 25 minutes (stc), or 18 minutes (pc), allowing the pressure cooker to release naturally. Let sit 5 minutes after cooking, stir and serve warm.

Recipe 45 *(Warming)*

You'll need:

1-2	Tbsp ghee
⅓	tsp mineral salt
¼	tsp cumin seeds
1	Tbsp cumin powder
½	tsp asafoetida powder
½	cup split mung beans
1½	cups water

Here's how:

Heat the ghee in a pot over medium heat. Then, add salt and cumin seeds; simmer until the aroma comes up to meet you. Next, add cumin and asafoetida powder and simmer until the aroma is present. Add split mung beans, stir to coat with ghee and spices and simmer for a few minutes. Add water, stir and bring to a boil; reduce to simmer and cover for 25 minutes (stc), or 18 minutes (pc), allowing the pressure cooker to release naturally. Let sit 5 minutes after cooking, stir and serve warm.

Recipe 46 *(Warming)*

You'll need:

2	Tbsp olive oil
⅓	tsp mineral salt
½	tsp cumin seeds
2	tsp raw carob powder
½	tsp fenugreek powder
½	cup split mung beans
1½	cups water
½	cup split mung beans
1 ½	cups water

Here's how:

Heat the oil in a pot over medium heat. Then, add salt and cumin seeds; simmer until the aroma comes up to meet you. Next, add carob and fenugreek powder and simmer until the aroma is present. Add split mung beans, stir to coat with oil and spices and simmer for a few minutes. Add water, stir and bring to a boil; reduce to simmer and cover for 25 minutes (stc), or 18 minutes (pc), allowing the pressure cooker to release naturally. Let sit 5 minutes after cooking, stir and serve warm.

Recipe 47 *(Warming)*

You'll need:

1	Tbsp sesame oil
1	Tbsp ghee
⅓	tsp mineral salt
1	tsp grated fresh turmeric
¼	tsp black pepper
¼	tsp asafoetida powder
1	tsp coriander powder
1	tsp fresh lime juice
½	cup split mung beans
2	cups water

Here's how:

Heat the oil in a pot over medium heat. Then, add salt, fresh turmeric and black pepper; simmer until the aroma comes up to meet you. Next, add asafoetida and coriander powders; simmer until the aroma is present. Add split mung beans, stir to coat with ghee and spices and simmer for a few minutes. Add water, stir and bring to a boil; reduce to simmer and cover for 25 minutes (stc), or 18 minutes (pc), allowing the pressure cooker to release naturally. Add the lime, stir and let sit 5 minutes after cooking. Serve warm. To make this a soup just add one to two more cups of water to the cooking process.

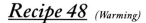

Recipe 48 *(Warming)*

You'll need:

1-2 Tbsp ghee
⅓ tsp mineral salt
2 tsp cumin powder
½ tsp turmeric powder
½ cup chopped fresh parsley
½ cup split mung beans
1½ cups water

Here's how:

Heat the ghee in a pot over medium heat. Then, add salt, cumin and turmeric powders; simmer until the aroma comes up to meet you. Next, add the parsley and simmer briefly. Add split mung beans, stir to coat with ghee and spices and simmer for a few minutes. Add water, stir and bring to a boil; reduce to simmer and cover for 25 minutes (stc), or 18 minutes (pc), allowing the pressure cooker to release naturally. Let sit 5 minutes after cooking, stir and serve warm.

Recipe 49 *(Warming)*

You'll need:

1-2 Tbsp ghee
⅓ tsp mineral salt
1 tsp cumin seeds
¼ tsp ground black pepper
1 Tbsp ground raw carob powder
½ cup split mung beans
1½ cups water

Here's how:

Heat the ghee in a pot over medium heat. Then, add salt, cumin, black pepper and carob powder; simmer until the aroma comes up to meet you. Next, add carob powder and simmer until the aroma is present. Add split mung beans, stir to coat with ghee and spices and simmer for a few minutes. Add water, stir and bring to a boil; reduce to simmer and cover for 25 minutes (stc), or 18 minutes (pc), allowing the pressure cooker to release naturally. Let sit 5 minutes after cooking, stir and serve warm.

Recipe 50 *(Warming)*

You'll need:

1-2	Tbsp ghee
⅓	tsp mineral salt
1	sweet cinnamon stick
¼	tsp cardamom seeds
1	tsp turmeric powder
½	tsp asafoetida powder
½	cup whole mung beans soaked in advance water

Here's how:

Heat the ghee in a pot over medium heat. Then, add salt, cinnamon and cardamom and simmer until the aroma comes up to meet you. Next, add turmeric and asafoetida and simmer until the aroma is present. Add mung beans, stir to coat with ghee and spices and simmer for a few minutes. Add water to cover, stir and bring to a boil; reduce to simmer and cover for 35-40 minutes (stc), or 25 minutes (pc), allowing the pressure cooker to release naturally. Let sit 5 minutes after cooking, stir and serve warm.

Recipe 51 *(Warming)*

You'll need:

1-2	Tbsp ghee
⅓	tsp mineral salt
1	tsp chopped fresh ginger root
½	tsp brown mustard seeds
1	tsp cardamom powder
1	tsp turmeric powder
½	cup split mung beans
2	cups water
1-2	tsp freshly ground saffron

Here's how:

Heat the ghee in a pot over medium heat. Then, add salt, ginger root and brown mustard seeds and simmer until the aroma comes up to meet you. Next, add cardamom and turmeric and simmer until the aroma is present. Add split mung beans, stir to coat with ghee and spices and simmer for a few minutes. Add water, stir and bring to a boil; reduce to simmer and cover for 25 minutes (stc), or 18 minutes (pc), allowing the pressure cooker to release naturally. Let sit 5 minutes after cooking, stir, dress with saffron and serve warm.

Recipe 52 *(Warming)*

You'll need:

1-2 Tbsp ghee
⅓ tsp mineral salt
½ tsp ground cumin seed
½ tsp cinnamon powder
½ tsp asafoetida
½ cup split mung beans
1½ cups water

Here's how:

Heat the ghee in a pot over medium heat. Then, add salt and cumin and simmer until the aroma comes up to meet you. Next add cinnamon and asafoetida powders until the aroma is present. Add split mung beans, stir to coat with ghee and spices and simmer for a few minutes. Add water, stir and bring to a boil; reduce to simmer and cover for 25 minutes (stc), or 18 minutes (pc), allowing the pressure cooker to release naturally. Let sit 5 minutes after cooking, stir and serve warm.

Recipe 53 *(Warming)*

You'll need:

1-2 Tbsp ghee
⅓ tsp mineral salt
½ tsp mustard seeds
¼ tsp cumin seeds
½ tsp cardamom powder
½ cup split mung beans
1½ cups water

Here's how:

Heat the ghee in a pot over medium heat. Then, add salt, mustard and cumin and simmer until the aroma comes up to meet you. Next add the cardamom powder and simmer until the aroma is present. Add split mung, stir to coat with ghee and spices and simmer for a few minutes. Add water, stir and bring to a boil; reduce to simmer and cover for 25 minutes (stc), or 18 minutes (pc), allowing the pressure cooker to release naturally. Let sit 5 minutes after cooking, stir and serve warm.

Recipe 54 *(Warming)*

You'll need:

1-2	Tbsp ghee
⅓	tsp mineral salt
¾	tsp fresh chopped ginger root
½	tsp cumin seed
¾	tsp fennel powder
¼	cup fresh chopped parsley
½	cup split mung beans
1½	cups water

Here's how:

Heat the ghee in a pot over medium heat. Then, add salt, ginger and cumin and simmer until the aroma comes up to meet you. Next add the fennel powder and simmer until the aroma is present. Add split mung and parsley, stir to coat with ghee and spices and simmer for a few minutes. Add water, stir and bring to a boil; reduce to simmer and cover for 25 minutes (stc), or 18 minutes (pc), allowing the pressure cooker to release naturally. Let sit 5 minutes after cooking, stir and serve warm.

Recipe 55 *(Warming)*

You'll need:

1-2	Tbsp ghee
⅓	tsp mineral salt
½	tsp grated fresh ginger root
½	tsp grated fresh turmeric root
1	tsp coriander powder
¼	chopped fresh basil
½	cup split mung beans
1½	cups water

Here's how:

Heat the ghee in a pot over medium heat. Then, add salt, ginger and turmeric and simmer until the aroma comes up to meet you. Next add the coriander powder and fresh basil and simmer until the aroma is present. Add split mung beans, stir to coat with ghee and spices and simmer for a few minutes. Add water, stir and bring to a boil; reduce to simmer and cover for 25 minutes (stc), or 18 minutes (pc), allowing the pressure cooker to release naturally. Let sit 5 minutes after cooking, stir and serve warm.

Recipe 56 *(Warming +)*

You'll need:

1-2	Tbsp olive oil
⅓	tsp mineral salt
¾	tsp ginger powder
1	½ tsp raw carob powder
½	tsp cinnamon powder
¼	tsp asafoetida powder
½	cup split mung beans
2½	cups water

Here's how:

Heat the oil in a pot over medium heat. Then, add salt, ginger, carob, cinnamon and asafoetida powders; simmer until the aroma comes up to meet you. Add split mung beans, stir to coat with oil and spices and simmer for a few minutes. Add water, stir and bring to a boil; reduce to simmer and cover for 25 minutes (stc), or 18 minutes (pc), allowing the pressure cooker to release naturally. Let sit 5 minutes after cooking, stir and serve warm.

Recipe 57 *(Warming -)*

You'll need:

1-2	Tbsp ghee
⅓	tsp mineral salt
½	tsp chopped fresh ginger root
½	tsp chopped fresh turmeric root
½	tsp fenugreek powder
½	cup split mung beans
1½	cups water
¼	cup fresh cilantro

Here's how:

Heat the ghee in a pot over medium heat. Then, add salt, ginger and turmeric; simmer until the aroma comes up to meet you. Next add the fenugreek powder and simmer until the aroma is present. Add split mung beans, stir to coat with ghee and spices and simmer for a few minutes. Add water, stir and bring to a boil; reduce to simmer and cover for 25 minutes (stc), or 18 minutes (pc), allowing the pressure cooker to release naturally. Add the cilantro and let sit 5 minutes after cooking, stir and serve warm.

Recipe 58 *(Warming)*

You'll need:

1-2 Tbsp ghee
⅓ tsp mineral salt
8-10 rosemary seeds
¼ tsp fennel seeds
½ tsp cardamom powder
½ tsp fennel powder
½ tsp cinnamon
½ cup split mung beans
1½ cups water

Here's how:

Heat the ghee in a pot over medium heat. Then, add salt, rosemary and fennel seeds and simmer until the aroma comes up to meet you. Next add cardamom, fennel and cinnamon and simmer until the aroma is present. Add split mung beans, stir to coat with ghee and spices and simmer for a few minutes. Add water, stir and bring to a boil; reduce to simmer and cover for 25 minutes (stc), or 18 minutes (pc), allowing the pressure cooker to release naturally. Let sit for 5 minutes after cooking, stir and serve warm.

Recipe 59 *(Warming -)*

You'll need:

1-2 Tbsp ghee
⅓ tsp mineral salt
½ tsp fresh ginger root
¾ tsp ground coriander seeds
1 tsp fennel powder
¼ tsp fenugreek powder
1 Tbsp fresh chopped mint
½ cup split mung beans
1½ cups water

Here's how:

Heat the ghee in a pot over medium heat. Then, add salt, ginger and coriander and simmer until the aroma comes up to meet you. Next add the fennel and fenugreek until the aroma comes up. Add split mung beans, stir to coat with ghee and spices and simmer for a few minutes. Add water, stir and bring to a boil; reduce to simmer and cover for 25 minutes (stc), or 18 minutes (pc), allowing the pressure cooker to release naturally. Open, stir and add the mint and let sit for 5 minutes. Serve warm.

Recipe 60 *(Cooling)*

You'll need:

1-2	Tbsp ghee
⅓	tsp mineral salt
2	tsp raw carob powder
1	Tbsp coriander powder
2	tsp dried mint
½	cup split mung beans
1½	cups water

Here's how:

Heat the ghee in a pot over medium heat. Then, add salt, carob and coriander and simmer until the aroma comes up to meet you. Add split mung beans and mint, stir to coat with ghee and spices and simmer for a few minutes. Add water, stir and bring to a boil; reduce to simmer and cover for 25 minutes (stc), or 18 minutes (pc), allowing the pressure cooker to release naturally. Let sit 5 minutes after cooking, stir and serve warm.

Recipe 61 *(Cooling)*

You'll need:

1-2	Tbsp ghee
⅓	tsp mineral salt
½	tsp cardamom seeds
1	Tbsp coriander powder
¼	fresh chopped mint leaves
½	cup split mung beans
1½	cups water

Here's how:

Heat the ghee in a pot over medium heat. Then, add salt, cardamom and coriander and simmer until the aroma comes up to meet you. Add split mung beans and mint, stir to coat with ghee and spices and simmer for a few minutes. Add water, stir and bring to a boil; reduce to simmer and cover for 25 minutes (stc), or 18 minutes (pc), allowing the pressure cooker to release naturally. Let sit 5 minutes after cooking, stir and serve warm.

Mediterranean recipes

<u>*Recipe 62*</u>

Complete 60:40 balance bowl recipe

Augmenting 60% of meal: *Rice, summer squash*	***Extractive 40% of meal:*** *Mung beans, chard*

Preparation time: *10 minutes to get rice and mung beans cooking and chop the veggies then 10-15 minutes cooking time for veggies (25 minutes total).*	***Serves: 4***

Prepare the beans and rice first. Halfway through come back to cook the veggies and serve it all together in a beautiful meal.

Mung beans *(Warming)*

You'll need:

2	Tbsp olive oil
⅓	tsp mineral salt
1	tsp dried oregano
2	small bay leaves
1	tsp fresh lime juice
½	cup split mung beans
1½	cups water

Here's how:

Heat the oil in a pot over medium heat. Then, add salt, oregano and bay leaves and simmer until the aroma comes up to meet you. Add split mung beans; stir to coat with ghee and spices and simmer for a few minutes. Add water, stir and bring to a boil; reduce to simmer and cover for 25 minutes (stc), or 18 minutes (pc), allowing the pressure cooker to release naturally. Open and stir in lime and let sit for 5 minutes. Serve warm.

Arborio rice *(Neutral)*

You'll need:

1	cup white arborio rice
2	tsp ghee
⅓	tsp mineral salt
¼	tsp saffron (optional)
2	cups water

Here's how:

Heat the oil in a small pot and add the rice and stir, simmering for 1-2 minutes. Grind the saffron in 2 Tbsp hot water and add to the rice. Add the water, stir, cover and simmer for 35 minutes until the water is absorbed. Turn off the heat and let sit for 5 minutes before serving. This can also be cooked in a rice cooker, pressure cooker or clay pot with appropriate time adjustments.

<u>*Recipe 62 continued*</u>

Complete 60:40 balance bowl recipe

Summer squash *(Warming)*

You'll need:

2-3   medium summer squash chopped
1   Tbsp olive oil
⅓   tsp mineral salt
½   tsp cumin seeds ground
2   tsp chopped basil
¼   tsp turmeric powder
Water to ¼ height of veggie

Here's how:

Heat the oil in a small pan and simmer the salt and cumin until the aroma is present. Add in the basil and simmer briefly. Add the squash and stir to cover with the oil and spices. Add the water, stir, cover and simmer until tender and can be pierced with a knife. Turn off the heat and add the coriander. Cover and let sit for 5 minutes.

Chard *(Warming -)*

You'll need:

4   cups fresh chopped chard
2   Tbsp olive oil
¾   tsp mineral salt
1   tsp grated ginger root
½   tsp celery seed
Water to ¼ height of veggie

Here's how:

Heat the oil in a small pan and simmer the salt, ginger and celery seed until the aroma is present. Add the greens and stir to cover with the oil and spices. Add water, stir, cover and simmer until tender. Turn off the heat let sit for 5 minutes.

Recipe 63 *(Warming)*

You'll need:

2	Tbsp olive oil
⅓	tsp mineral salt
¼	tsp fennel seed
½	tsp black sesame seeds
1	tsp cumin powder
¼	tsp asafoetida powder
½	tsp dried oregano
1	tsp fresh lime juice
½	cup split mung beans
2	cups water

Here's how:

Heat the oil in a pot over medium heat. Then, add salt, fennel and sesame seeds and simmer until the aroma comes up to meet you. Next add cumin, asafoetida, oregano and basil and simmer until the aroma is present. Add split mung beans and lime juice; stir to coat with ghee and spices and simmer for a few minutes. Add water, stir and bring to a boil; reduce to simmer and cover for 25 minutes (stc), or 18 minutes (pc), allowing the pressure cooker to release naturally. Let sit 5 minutes after cooking, stir and serve warm.

Recipe 64 *(Warming)*

You'll need:

1	Tbsp olive oil
1	Tbsp ghee
⅓	tsp mineral salt
½	tsp cumin seed
¾	tsp cardamom powder
¼	tsp asafoetida powder
1	Tbsp fresh chopped Italian basil
½	cup split mung beans
2	cups water

Here's how:

Heat the oil and ghee in a pot over medium heat. Then, add salt and cumin and simmer until the aroma comes up to meet you. Next add cardamom, asafoetida and basil and simmer until the aroma is present. Add split mung beans; stir to coat with ghee and spices and simmer for a few minutes. Add water, stir and bring to a boil; reduce to simmer and cover for 25 minutes (stc), or 18 minutes (pc), allowing the pressure cooker to release naturally. Let sit 5 minutes after cooking, stir and serve warm.

Recipe 65 *(Warming)*

You'll need:

1	Tbsp olive oil
1	Tbsp ghee
⅓	tsp mineral salt
¼	tsp ground black pepper
½	tsp dried oregano
1	Tbsp dried or fresh parsley
½	cup split mung beans
2	cups water

Here's how:

Heat the oil and ghee in a pot over medium heat. Then, add salt and black pepper and simmer until the aroma comes up to meet you. Next add oregano and parsley and simmer until the aroma is present. Add split mung beans; stir to coat with ghee and spices and simmer for a few minutes. Add water, stir and bring to a boil; reduce to simmer and cover for 25 minutes (stc), or 18 minutes (pc), allowing the pressure cooker to release naturally. Let sit 5 minutes after cooking, stir and serve warm.

Recipe 66 *(Warming)*

You'll need:

1	Tbsp olive oil
1	Tbsp ghee
⅓	tsp mineral salt
¼	tsp ground black pepper
½	tsp rosemary
½	tsp thyme
½	cup whole mung beans
Squeeze of fresh lemon	
Water	

Here's how:

Heat the oil and ghee in a pot over medium heat. Then, add salt and black pepper and simmer until the aroma comes up to meet you. Next add rosemary and thyme and simmer until the aroma is present. Add whole mung beans; stir to coat with ghee and spices and simmer for a few minutes. Add water to cover, stir and bring to a boil; reduce to simmer and cover for 35-40 minutes (stc), or 25 minutes (pc), allowing the pressure cooker to release naturally. Let sit 5 minutes after cooking, add a small squeeze of lemon, stir and serve warm. To make this into a spread for a roll up use a little less water and mash or blend with the cooking water to make a hummus type spread.

Recipe 67 *(Warming)*

You'll need:

1	Tbsp olive oil
1	Tbsp ghee
⅓	tsp mineral salt
1	tsp grated fresh turmeric root
½	tsp dill seed
½	tsp sumac powder
1	Tbsp coriander powder
½	cup split mung beans
2	cups water

Here's how:

Heat the oil and ghee in a pot over medium heat. Then, add salt, fresh turmeric and dill seed and simmer until the aroma comes up to meet you. Next add sumac and coriander powders and simmer until the aroma is present. Add split mung beans; stir to coat with ghee and spices and simmer for a few minutes. Add water, stir and bring to a boil; reduce to simmer and cover for 25 minutes (stc), or 18 minutes (pc), allowing the pressure cooker to release naturally. Let sit 5 minutes after cooking, stir and serve warm.

Recipe 68 *(Warming +)*

You'll need:

1	Tbsp sesame oil
1	Tbsp ghee
⅓	tsp mineral salt
1	tsp grated fresh ginger root
½	tsp fenugreek seed
¼	tsp clove powder
1	pinch nutmeg powder
½	cup split mung beans
2	cups water

Here's how:

Heat the oil and ghee in a pot over medium heat. Then, add salt, fresh ginger and fenugreek and simmer until the aroma comes up to meet you. Next add clove and nutmeg and simmer until the aroma is present. Add split mung beans; stir to coat with ghee, oil and spices and simmer for a few minutes. Add water, stir and bring to a boil; reduce to simmer and cover for 25 minutes (stc), or 18 minutes (pc), allowing the pressure cooker to release naturally. Let sit 5 minutes after cooking, stir and serve warm.

Recipe 69 *(Warming +)*

You'll need:

2	Tbsp sesame oil
⅓	tsp mineral salt
¾	tsp cumin seed
½	tsp ground coriander seed
½	tsp brown mustard seed
1	large bay leaf
½	cup split mung beans
2	cups water

Here's how:

Heat the oil in a pot over medium heat. Then, add salt, cumin, coriander, brown mustard seeds and bay leaf and simmer until the aroma comes up to meet you. Add split mung beans; stir to coat with oil and spices and simmer for a few minutes. Add water, stir and bring to a boil; reduce to simmer and cover for 25 minutes (stc), or 18 minutes (pc), allowing the pressure cooker to release naturally. Let sit 5 minutes after cooking, stir and serve warm.

Recipe 70 *(Warming +)*

You'll need:

1-2	Tbsp ghee
⅓	tsp mineral salt
½	tsp rosemary
¼	tsp ground black pepper
½	tsp asafoetida powder
1	Tbsp chopped fresh parsley
½	cup split mung beans
2	cups water

Here's how:

Heat the ghee in a pot over medium heat. Then, add salt, rosemary and asafoetida and simmer until the aroma comes up to meet you. Next add parsley and simmer until the aroma is present. Add split mung beans; stir to coat with ghee and spices and simmer for a few minutes. Add water, stir and bring to a boil; reduce to simmer and cover for 25 minutes (stc), or 18 minutes (pc), allowing the pressure cooker to release naturally. Let sit 5 minutes after cooking, stir and serve warm.

Recipe 71 *(Warming +)*

You'll need:

1-2	Tbsp	ghee
⅓	tsp	mineral salt
1	tsp	ground sesame seeds
¾	tsp	turmeric powder
1	Tbsp	chopped fresh basil
½	cup	split mung beans
2	cups	water

Here's how:

Heat the ghee in a pot over medium heat. Then, add salt and sesame seeds and simmer until the aroma comes up to meet you. Next add turmeric powder and basil and simmer until the aroma is present. Add split mung beans; stir to coat with ghee and spices and simmer for a few minutes. Add water, stir and bring to a boil; reduce to simmer and cover for 25 minutes (stc), or 18 minutes (pc), allowing the pressure cooker to release naturally. Let sit 5 minutes after cooking, stir and serve warm.

Recipe 72 *(Warming)*

You'll need:

1-2	Tbsp	ghee
⅓	tsp	mineral salt
½	tsp	dill seeds
¾	tsp	turmeric powder
1	tsp	coriander powder
¼	tsp	fenugreek powder
½	cup	split mung beans
½	tsp	ground golpar
1½	cups	water

Here's how:

Heat the ghee in a pot over medium heat. Then, add salt and dill seeds and simmer until the aroma comes up to meet you. Next add turmeric, coriander and asafoetida powders and simmer until the aroma is present. Add split mung beans; stir to coat with ghee and spices and simmer for a few minutes. Add water, stir and bring to a boil; reduce to simmer and cover for 25 minutes (stc), or 18 minutes (pc), allowing the pressure cooker to release naturally. Let sit 5 minutes after cooking, stir, top with golpar and serve warm.

Recipe 73 *(Warming)*

You'll need:

1-2	Tbsp ghee
⅓	tsp mineral salt
½	tsp fenugreek seeds
¾	tsp dried oregano
½	tsp dried thyme
1	Tbsp chopped fresh parsley
½	cup split mung beans
1½	cups water

Here's how:

Heat the ghee in a pot over medium heat. Then, add salt and fenugreek seeds and simmer until the aroma comes up to meet you. Next add oregano and thyme and simmer until the aroma is present. Add split mung beans; stir to coat with ghee and spices and simmer for a few minutes. Add water, stir and bring to a boil; reduce to simmer and cover for 25 minutes (stc), or 18 minutes (pc), allowing the pressure cooker to release naturally. Open and stir in the parsley. Let sit 5 minutes after cooking, stir and serve warm.

Recipe 74 *(Warming)*

You'll need:

2	Tbsp olive oil
⅓	tsp mineral salt
1	tsp dried basil
½	tsp dried oregano
1	tsp coriander powder
¼	tsp asafoetida powder
½	cup split mung beans
1½	cups water

Here's how:

Heat the oil in a pot over medium heat. Then, add salt basil, oregano, coriander and asafoetida and simmer until the aroma comes up to meet you. Add split mung beans; stir to coat with oil and spices and simmer for a few minutes. Add water, stir and bring to a boil; reduce to simmer and cover for 25 minutes (stc), or 18 minutes (pc), allowing the pressure cooker to release naturally. Let sit 5 minutes after cooking, stir and serve warm.

Recipe 75 *(Warming)*

You'll need:

2	Tbsp olive oil
⅓	tsp mineral salt
1	tsp chopped fresh ginger
1	tsp coriander powder
¼	tsp asafoetida
½	cup split mung beans
2	cups water

Here's how:

Heat the oil in a pot over medium heat. Then, add salt and ginger and simmer until the aroma comes up to meet you. Next add coriander and asafoetida and simmer until the aroma is present. Add split mung beans; stir to coat with oil and spices and simmer for a few minutes. Add water, stir and bring to a boil; reduce to simmer and cover for 25 minutes (stc), or 18 minutes (pc), allowing the pressure cooker to release naturally. Let sit 5 minutes after cooking, stir and serve warm.

Recipe 76 *(Warming)*

You'll need:

1-2	Tbsp ghee
⅓	tsp mineral salt
½	tsp grated ginger root
½	tsp grated turmeric root
½	tsp dill seed
1	Tbsp coriander powder
½	tsp fenugreek powder
½	cup split mung beans
¼	cup chopped fresh dill
1½	cups water

Here's how:

Heat the ghee in a pot over medium heat. Then, add salt, ginger and turmeric, and dill seeds and simmer until the aroma comes up to meet you. Next add coriander and fenugreek powders and simmer until the aroma is present. Add split mung beans; stir to coat with ghee and spices and simmer for a few minutes. Add water, stir and bring to a boil; reduce to simmer and cover for 25 minutes (stc), or 18 minutes (pc), allowing the pressure cooker to release naturally. Let sit 5 minutes after cooking, stir, dress with fresh dill and serve warm.

Recipe 77 *(Warming)*

You'll need:

1	Tbsp ghee
1	Tbsp olive oil
⅓	tsp mineral salt
1	tsp fresh chopped ginger
½	tsp fenugreek powder
1	tsp dried or 2 tsp fresh basil
½	cup split mung beans
4	cups water

Here's how:

Heat the ghee and oil in a pot over medium heat. Then, add salt and ginger and simmer until the aroma comes up to meet you. Next add fenugreek powder and basil and simmer until the aroma is present. Add split mung beans; stir to coat with ghee and spices and simmer for a few minutes. Add water, stir and bring to a boil; reduce to simmer and cover for 25 minutes (stc), or 18 minutes (pc), allowing the pressure cooker to release naturally. Let sit 5 minutes after cooking, stir and serve warm.

Recipe 78 *(Warming +)*

You'll need:

2	Tbsp sesame oil
⅓	tsp mineral salt
1	tsp chopped ginger root
¾	tsp fenugreek powder
½	cup split mung beans
1½	cups water
2	Tbsp fresh chopped basil
Squeeze of fresh lemon juice	

Here's how:

Heat the oil in a pot over medium heat. Then, add salt and ginger and simmer until the aroma comes up to meet you. Next add fenugreek powder and simmer until the aroma is present. Add split mung beans; stir to coat with oil and spices and simmer for a few minutes. Add water, stir and bring to a boil; reduce to simmer and cover for 25 minutes (stc), or 18 minutes (pc), allowing the pressure cooker to release naturally. Open and stir in the basil and a squeeze of lemon. Let sit 5 minutes after cooking, stir and serve warm.

Recipe 79 (Neutral)

You'll need:

2	Tbsp sunflower oil
⅓	tsp mineral salt
½	tsp grated ginger root
1	tsp coriander powder
1	tsp fennel powder
¼	tsp ground black pepper
½	cup split mung beans
2	cups water

Small handful of chopped fresh mint

Here's how:

Heat the oil in a pot over medium heat. Then, add salt and ginger and simmer until the aroma comes up to meet you. Next add coriander and fennel powders and black pepper and simmer until the aroma is present. Add split mung beans; stir to coat with oil and spices and simmer for a few minutes. Add water, stir and bring to a boil; reduce to simmer and cover for 25 minutes (stc), or 18 minutes (pc), allowing the pressure cooker to release naturally. Let sit 5 minutes after cooking, stir, dress with mint and serve warm.

Recipe 80 (Cooling)

You'll need:

2	Tbsp sunflower oil
⅓	tsp mineral salt
½	tsp ground coriander seeds
½	tsp brown mustard seeds
1	tsp fennel powder
¼	tsp asafoetida powder
2	cups chopped beet greens
½	cup split mung beans
2	cups water
¼	cup chopped cilantro

Here's how:

Heat the oil in a pot over medium heat. Then, add salt, coriander and mustard seeds and simmer until the aroma comes up to meet you. Next add fennel and asafoetida powders and beet greens and simmer until the aroma is present. Add split mung beans; stir to coat with oil and spices and simmer for a few minutes. Add water, stir and bring to a boil; reduce to simmer and cover for 25 minutes (stc), or 18 minutes (pc), allowing the pressure cooker to release naturally. Open and stir in cilantro. Let sit 5 minutes after cooking, stir and serve warm.

Recipe 81 *(Neutral)*

You'll need:

1-2	Tbsp ghee
⅓	tsp mineral salt
½	tsp chopped ginger root
1	tsp coriander powder
½	tsp fenugreek powder
½	cup split mung beans
¼	cup fresh chopped genovese basil
4	cups water

Here's how:

Heat the ghee in a pot over medium heat. Then, add salt and ginger and simmer until the aroma comes up to meet you. Next add coriander and fenugreek powders and simmer until the aroma is present. Add split mung beans; stir to coat with oil and spices and simmer for a few minutes. Add water, stir and bring to a boil; reduce to simmer and cover for 25 minutes (stc), or 18 minutes (pc), allowing the pressure cooker to release naturally. Open and stir in basil. Let sit 5 minutes after cooking, stir and serve warm.

Recipe 82 *(Neutral)*

You'll need:

2	Tbsp sunflower oil
⅓	tsp mineral salt
½	tsp grated ginger root
½	tsp dill seed
2	tsp coriander powder
½	tsp turmeric powder
½	cup split mung beans
2	cups water
¼	cup chopped cilantro

Pinch ground black pepper

Here's how:

Heat the oil in a pot over medium heat. Then, add salt, ginger and dill seed and simmer until the aroma comes up to meet you. Next add coriander and turmeric powders and black pepper and simmer until the aroma is present. Add split mung beans; stir to coat with oil and spices and simmer for a few minutes. Add water, stir and bring to a boil; reduce to simmer and cover for 25 minutes (stc), or 18 minutes (pc), allowing the pressure cooker to release naturally. Let sit 5 minutes after cooking, stir and serve warm.

Mexican recipes

Recipe 83

Complete 60:40 balance bowl recipe

Augmenting 60% of meal: *Mini tortilla and/or rice, paneer, sweet potato*	**Extractive 40% of meal:** *Split mung dhal, red cabbage*
Preparation time: *10 minutes to get rice and mung beans cooking and chop the veggies then 10-15 minutes cooking time for veggies.*	**Serves:** *4*

Prepare the beans and rice first (25 minutes total). Halfway through come back to cook the veggies and serve it all together in a beautiful meal.

Split mung dhal (Neutral)

You'll need:

1-2 Tbsp ghee
⅓ tsp mineral salt
1 tsp grated ginger root
1 tsp coriander powder
1 tsp cumin powder
½ cup split mung beans
1 ½ cups water
1 Tbsp chopped cilantro
Zest of lime

Here's how:

Heat the ghee in a pot over medium heat. Then, add salt and ginger and simmer until the aroma comes up to meet you. Next add coriander and cumin powders and simmer until the aroma is present. Add split mung beans; stir to coat with ghee and spices and simmer for a few minutes. Add water, stir and bring to a boil; reduce to simmer and cover for 25 minutes (stc), or 18 minutes (pc), allowing the pressure cooker to release naturally. Open and stir in lime and cilantro. Let sit 5 minutes after cooking, stir and serve warm.

Brown and white rice

You'll need:

½ cup white and ½ cup brown rice
2 tsp ghee
⅓ tsp mineral salt
½ tsp ground fennel seeds
2 cups water

Here's how:

Heat the ghee in a pot and simmer the salt and fennel until the aroma is present. Add the rice and stir, simmering for 1-2 minutes. Add the water, stir, cover and simmer for 35 minutes until the water is absorbed and the barley is plump and softish. Turn off the heat and let sit for 5 minutes before serving. This can also be cooked in a rice cooker, pressure cooker or clay pot with appropriate time adjustments.

<u>*Recipe 83 continued*</u>

Complete 60:40 balance bowl recipe

Sweet potato *(Warming)*

You'll need:

2	medium sweet potato cut in quarters thumb length
1	Tbsp ghee
⅓	tsp mineral salt
½	tsp cumin seeds ground
½	tsp fennel seeds ground
¼	tsp turmeric powder

Water to ¼ height of veggie
Chopped coriander leaves

Here's how:

Heat the oil in a small pan and simmer the salt, cumin, and fennel until the aroma is present. Add in the turmeric and simmer briefly. Add the sweet potato to a baking dish and pour the oil and spices over the potatoes. Add water, stir, and bake at 190C or 375F until tender and can be pierced with a knife, about 20 minutes. Turn off the heat and add the coriander. Remove from the oven and let sit for 5 minutes.

Red cabbage *(Neutral)*

You'll need:

4	cups fresh chopped red cabbage
2	Tbsp olive oil
¾	tsp mineral salt
½	tsp ground coriander seeds
⅛	tsp black pepper
½	cup fresh cheese

Water to ¼ height of veggie

Here's how:

Heat the oil in a small pan and simmer the salt, coriander, and pepper until the aroma is present. Add the cabbage and stir to cover with the oil and spices. Add water, stir, cover and simmer until tender. Turn off the heat and add the paneer. Cover and let sit for 5 minutes.

Recipe 83 continued

Complete 60:40 balance bowl recipe

Mini tortilla *(Warming -)*

You'll need:

¾   cup whole wheat or spelt flour
½   cup rice flour (teff flour is
       another option)
⅓   tsp mineral salt
1   Tbsp ghee (a bit more for cooking)
½-¾ cup water (the amount will vary
       by the season, climate, and grind
       of the flour)

Here's how:

Stir flour, mineral salt, and melted ghee together. Add water slowly and combine well until the dough is consistently mixed and slightly sticky (use your hands for the best results).

Break off golf-ball-sized pieces and roll them into 8 small balls using the palms of your hands. Set the balls aside in order, so that you can roll out the oldest one first. It is helpful for the dough balls to sit a few minutes, but not too long or they will dry out. Warm a pan over medium heat while you begin rolling the balls. If you don't have a roller, using the side of a jar or fingers can work fine.

Sprinkle flour on a cutting board, rolling mat or clean countertop. Place the first ball in the middle of the flour and flatten the ball with your palm to press it down. Sprinkle flour on top. Roll each ball into a small round, moving it in a clockwise motion as you roll. Don't worry if they aren't perfectly round, they taste just as great. If it gets sticky while you're rolling, sprinkle a little more flour on top.

Add 1 tsp. ghee to the warm pan and place the first 3 in the pan to cook while you roll the others (rolling right next to the cooktop is ideal). Cook for 1-3 minutes on each side. The time will depend on your pan and cooktop. They are easy to turn with your fingers or you can use a spatula. Add a few more drops of ghee to the pan before adding the next group.

Recipe 84 *(Warming)*

You'll need:

1-2	Tbsp	ghee
⅓	tsp	mineral salt
1	tsp	chopped ginger root
½	tsp	cumin seeds
½	tsp	cinnamon powder
⅛	tsp	clove powder
½	cup	split mung beans
1½	cups	water

Here's how:

Heat the ghee in a pot over medium heat. Then, add salt, ginger and cumin seeds and simmer until the aroma comes up to meet you. Next add cinnamon and clove powders and simmer until the aroma is present. Add split mung beans; stir to coat with ghee and spices and simmer for a few minutes. Add water, stir and bring to a boil; reduce to simmer and cover for 25 minutes (stc), or 18 minutes (pc), allowing the pressure cooker to release naturally. Let sit 5 minutes after cooking, stir and serve warm.

Recipe 85 *(Warming)*

You'll need:

1-2	Tbsp	ghee
⅓	tsp	mineral salt
½	tsp	grated ginger root
½	tsp	cumin seeds
⅛	tsp	anise seeds
½	tsp	coriander powder
½	cup	split mung beans
1½	cups	water
Pinch of clove powder		

Here's how:

Heat the ghee in a pot over medium heat. Then, add salt, ginger, cumin and anise seeds and simmer until the aroma comes up to meet you. Next add coriander and clove powders and simmer until the aroma is present. Add split mung beans; stir to coat with ghee and spices and simmer for a few minutes. Add water, stir and bring to a boil; reduce to simmer and cover for 25 minutes (stc), or 18 minutes (pc), allowing the pressure cooker to release naturally. Let sit 5 minutes after cooking, stir and serve warm.

Recipe 86 *(Warming)*

You'll need:

2	Tbsp olive oil
⅓	tsp mineral salt
¾	tsp grated ginger root
¼	tsp cumin seeds
1	tsp dried oregano
½	cup split mung beans
1¼	cups water

Pinch of ground black pepper
Small squeeze of lime

Here's how:

Heat the oil in a pot over medium heat. Then, add salt, ginger, cumin and black pepper and simmer until the aroma comes up to meet you. Next add oregano and simmer until the aroma is present. Add split mung beans; stir to coat with oil and spices and simmer for a few minutes. Add water, stir and bring to a boil; reduce to simmer and cover for 25 minutes (stc), or 18 minutes (pc), allowing the pressure cooker to release naturally. Open and stir in a small squeeze of lime. Let sit 5minutes after cooking, stir and serve warm.

Recipe 87 *(Warming)*

You'll need:

1-2	Tbsp ghee
⅓	tsp mineral salt
½	tsp grated ginger root
¼	tsp cumin seeds
¼	tsp cardamom seeds
¼	tsp anise seeds
¼	tsp cinnamon powder
¼	tsp coriander powder
¼	tsp fennel powder
½	cup split mung beans
4	cups water

Here's how:

Heat the ghee in a pot over medium heat. Then, add salt, ginger, cumin, cardamom and anise seeds and simmer until the aroma comes up to meet you. Next add coriander and fennel powders and simmer until the aroma is present. Add split mung beans; stir to coat with ghee and spices and simmer for a few minutes. Add water, stir and bring to a boil; reduce to simmer and cover for 25 minutes (stc), or 18 minutes (pc), allowing the pressure cooker to release naturally. Let sit 5 minutes after cooking, stir and serve warm.

Recipe 88 *(Warming -)*

You'll need:

1-2 Tbsp ghee
⅓ tsp mineral salt
¼ tsp grated ginger root
½ tsp fennel seeds
1 Tbsp coriander powder
¼ tsp asafoetida powder
¼ tsp fenugreek powder
½ cup split mung beans
2 cups water

Here's how:

Heat the ghee in a pot over medium heat. Then, add salt, ginger and fennel and simmer until the aroma comes up to meet you. Next add coriander, asafoetida and fenugreek powders and simmer until the aroma is present. Add split mung beans; stir to coat with ghee and spices and simmer for a few minutes. Add water, stir and bring to a boil; reduce to simmer and cover for 25 minutes (stc), or 18 minutes (pc), allowing the pressure cooker to release naturally. Let sit 5 minutes after cooking, stir and serve warm.

Recipe 89 *(Warming)*

You'll need:

1-2 Tbsp ghee
⅓ tsp mineral salt
¾ tsp cumin seeds
¼ tsp mustard seeds
1 thumbnail length of cinnamon bark stick
1 tsp coriander powder
½ cup whole mung beans
¼ cup fresh chopped cilantro
Water

Here's how:

Heat the ghee in a pot over medium heat. Then, add salt, cumin and mustard seeds and simmer until the aroma comes up to meet you. Next add cinnamon stick and coriander powders and simmer until the aroma is present. Add mung beans; stir to coat with ghee and spices and simmer for a few minutes. Add water to cover, stir and bring to a boil; reduce to simmer and cover for 35 - 40 minutes (stc), or 25 minutes (pc), allowing the pressure cooker to release naturally. Open and sprinkle the cilantro on top. Let sit 5 minutes after cooking, stir and serve warm.

Recipe 90 *(Neutral)*

You'll need:

1	Tbsp ghee
1	Tbsp coconut oil
⅓	tsp mineral salt
1	tsp fresh chopped ginger root
½	tsp fennel seeds
¼	tsp asafoetida powder
10-15	dried rose petals
½	tsp chopped fresh mint leaves
1	Tbsp chopped fresh cilantro
½	cup split mung beans
2	cups water

Here's how:

Heat the ghee and oil in a pot over medium heat. Then, add salt, ginger and fennel and simmer until the aroma comes up to meet you. Next add asafoetida powder, rose petals, mint and cilantro and simmer until the aroma is present. Add split mung beans; stir to coat with ghee and spices and simmer for a few minutes. Add water, stir and bring to a boil; reduce to simmer and cover for 25 minutes (stc), or 18 minutes (pc), allowing the pressure cooker to release naturally. Let sit 5 minutes after cooking, stir and serve warm.

Recipe 91 *(Cooling)*

You'll need:

1	Tbsp ghee
1	Tbsp sunflower oil
⅓	tsp mineral salt
¼	tsp fresh chopped ginger root
½	tsp cumin seeds
½	tsp coriander seeds
¼	tsp fennel seeds
½	tsp chopped fresh mint leaves
1	tsp chopped fresh cilantro
1	tsp chopped fresh parsley
½	cup split mung beans
1½	cups water

Here's how:

Heat the ghee and oil in a pot over medium heat. Then, add salt, ginger, cumin, coriander and fennel and simmer until the aroma comes up to meet you. Next add mint, cilantro and parsley and simmer until the aroma is present. Add split mung beans; stir to coat with ghee and oil and spices and simmer for a few minutes. Add water, stir and bring to a boil; reduce to simmer and cover for 25 minutes (stc), or 18 minutes (pc), allowing the pressure cooker to release naturally. Let sit 5 minutes after cooking, stir and serve warm.

Recipe 92 *(Cooling)*

You'll need:

1	Tbsp olive oil
1	Tbsp sunflower oil
⅓	tsp mineral salt
½	tsp fresh chopped ginger root
½	tsp dried mint leaves
1	tsp dried basil
1	Tbsp fresh chopped cilantro
½	cup split mung beans
1½	cups water

Here's how:

Heat the oil in a pot over medium heat. Then, add salt and ginger and simmer until the aroma comes up to meet you. Next add mint, basil and cilantro and simmer until the aroma is present. Add split mung beans; stir to coat with oil and spices and simmer for a few minutes. Add water, stir and bring to a boil; reduce to simmer and cover for 25 minutes (stc), or 18 minutes (pc), allowing the pressure cooker to release naturally. Let sit 5 minutes after cooking, stir and serve warm.

New Zealand recipes

Recipe 93

Complete 60:40 balance bowl recipe

Augmenting 60% of meal: *Barley, parsnips and white jasmine rice*	***Extractive 40% of meal:*** *Split mung dhal and silverbeet (chard)*
Preparation time: *10 minutes to get rice and mung beans cooking and chop the veggies then 10 minutes cooking time for veggies while you make the pie pancakes and 10 minutes baking in the oven.*	***Serves:*** *4*

Serve it all together in a beautiful meal in about 35–40 minutes.

Split mung dhal *(Warming)*

You'll need:

1-2	Tbsp ghee
⅓	tsp mineral salt
1	Tbsp korengo or seaweed
½	tsp cumin seeds
¼	tsp fennel seeds
½	cup kowhitiwhiti or watercress
½	cup split mung beans
1½	cups water

Here's how:

Heat the ghee in a pot over medium heat. Then, add salt, seaweed, cumin, and fennel and simmer until the aroma comes up to meet you. Next add watercress and simmer until the aroma is present. Add split mung beans; stir to coat with ghee and spices and simmer for a few minutes. Add water, stir and bring to a boil; reduce to simmer and cover for 25 minutes (stc), or 18 minutes (pc), allowing the pressure cooker to release naturally. Let sit 5 minutes after cooking, stir and serve warm.

Barley and white jasmine rice *(Neutral)*

You'll need:

½	cup each of barley and white jasmine rice
2	tsp ghee
⅓	tsp mineral salt
2	cups water

Here's how:

Heat the oil in a small pot and simmer the salt and barley for 1-2 minutes. Add the water, stir, cover and simmer for 35-40 minutes until the water is absorbed and the barley is plump and softish. Turn off the heat and let sit for 5 minutes before serving. This can also be cooked in a rice cooker, pressure cooker or clay pot with appropriate time adjustments.

Recipe 93 continued

Complete 60:40 balance bowl recipe

Parsnips *(Warming -)*

You'll need:

1	Tbsp ghee
¼	tsp mineral salt
½	tsp grated fresh ginger root
¼	tsp turmeric powder
¼	tsp ground black pepper
2	large parsnips chopped
¼	cup chopped basil

Water to ¼ height of veggie

Here's how:

Heat the oil in a small pan and simmer the salt and ginger until the aroma is present. Add in the turmeric and black pepper and simmer briefly. Add the parsnips and stir to cover with the oil and spices. Add the water, stir, cover and simmer until tender and can be pierced with a knife. Turn off the heat and add the basil. Cover and let sit for 5 minutes.

Silverbeet (chard) *(Warming)*

You'll need:

2	Tbsp olive oil
¾	tsp mineral salt
1	tsp ground white sesame seeds
2	Tbsp chopped walnuts
4	cups fresh chopped silverbeet

Water to ¼ height of veggie

Here's how:

Heat the oil in a small pan and simmer the salt, sesame, and walnuts until the aroma is present. Add the silverbeet and stir to cover with the oil and spices. Add water, stir, cover and simmer until tender. Turn off the heat and let sit for 5 minutes.

Recipe 93

Complete 60:40 balance bowl recipe

Veggie pie wrap *(Neutral)*

You'll need:

3	cups whole wheat flour
½	tsp mineral salt
2	Tbsp ghee (plus some for cooking)
½-1	cup water (the amount depends on the season and climate)

Here's how:

Stir flour, mineral salt, and ghee together. Add water, ¼ cup at a time, and using your hands, combine well until the dough is thoroughly mixed and slightly sticky.

Make 4 pieces and roll them into balls with the palms of your hands. Set the balls aside in order, so that you can roll out the oldest one first. It is helpful for the dough balls to sit a few minutes.

Sprinkle some flour on a cutting board, rolling mat or clean countertop. Place the first ball in the middle of the flour and flatten the ball with your palm to make an even surface. Sprinkle a bit of flour on top. With a rolling pin, roll each ball into a thin pancake, spinning the ball in a clockwise motion as you go. If it gets sticky while you're rolling, just sprinkle a little more flour on top.

Place parsnip and silverbeet into the center of each pancake and wrap into a square shape so that the edges overlap a bit and can be gently pressed together. Place them on a stainless steel cookie sheet or ceramic baking dish and bake in the oven for 10 minutes at 190C or 375F until the dough becomes firm. Use a spatula to serve. A variation is to put the grain and a thick dhal into the pie and serve the veggies on the side.

Vietnamese recipes

Recipe 94

Complete 60:40 balance bowl recipe

Augmenting 60% of meal: *Carrot and white basmati rice*	**Extractive 40% of meal:** *Purple cabbage, split mung and broccoli*
Preparation time: *10 minutes to get rice and mung beans cooking and chop the veggies then 10-15 minutes cooking time for veggies (25 minutes total).*	**Serves:** *4*

Give the vegetables a few minutes to cool for making wraps. Serve it all together in a beautiful meal or have each person make their own wraps.

Dhal soup (*Warming*)

You'll need:

1-2 Tbsp ghee
⅓ tsp mineral salt
1 tsp cumin powder
1 tsp coriander powder
½ tsp asafoetida powder
1 Tbsp chopped Thai basil
½ cup whole mung beans
¼ cup fresh chopped cilantro
2 ¼ - 2 ½ cups water

Here's how:

Heat the ghee in a pot over medium heat. Then, add salt, cumin, coriander and asafoetida powders and simmer until the aroma comes up to meet you. Next add basil and simmer until the aroma is present. Add mung beans; stir to coat with ghee and spices and simmer for a few minutes. Add water to cover, stir and bring to a boil; reduce to simmer and cover for 35-40 minutes (stc), or 25 minutes (pc), allowing the pressure cooker to release naturally. For a smooth consistency use a hand blender for 1-2 minutes. Sprinkle the cilantro on top. Let sit for 5 minutes and serve warm.

Rice (*Neutral*)

You'll need:

½ cup brown jasmine rice
½ cup white jasmine rice
2 tsp ghee
⅓ tsp mineral salt
2 cups water

Here's how:

Heat the oil in a small pot with the salt and add the rice and stir, simmering for 1-2 minutes. Add the water, stir, cover and simmer for 35 minutes until the water is absorbed and the brown rice is plump and softish. Turn off the heat and let sit 5 minutes before serving. This can also be cooked in a rice cooker, pressure cooker or clay pot with appropriate time adjustments.

Recipe 94 continued

Complete 60:40 balance bowl recipe

Shredded carrot and purple cabbage *(Cooling)*

You'll need:

4	medium carrots shredded
1	Tbsp ghee
½	tsp mineral salt
½	tsp chopped ginger root
1	tsp fennel seeds ground
4	cups shredded cabbage

Water to ¼ height of veggie
Chopped coriander leaves

Here's how:

Heat the oil in a small pan and simmer the salt, fennel, and ginger until the aroma is present. Add the cabbage and carrots and stir to cover with the oil and spices. Add the water, stir, cover and simmer until tender and can be pierced with a knife. Turn off the heat and add the coriander. Cover and let sit for 5 minutes.

Broccoli *(Warming +)*

You'll need:

4	cups fresh chopped broccoli
2	Tbsp sesame oil
½	tsp mineral salt
¼	tsp cayenne pepper
¼	lime

Water to ¼ height of veggie

Here's how:

Heat the oil in a small pan and add the salt and cayenne. Add the broccoli and stir to cover with the oil and spices. Add water, stir, cover and simmer until tender. Turn off the heat and add a small squeeze of lime. Cover and let sit for 5 minutes.

Recipe 94
Complete 60:40 balance bowl recipe

Rice wraps

You'll need:

4   rice wraps
All cooked ingredients

Here's how:

One at a time, soak rice wraps in hot water until slightly soft. Be sure not to soak too long or the wrap will tear. Remove and place on cutting board or plate and add the items you desire in your wrap (rice, dhal, and veggies).

Recipe 95 *(Warming)*

You'll need:

1-2	Tbsp ghee
⅓	tsp mineral salt
3	finger length pieces sea palm or other seaweed
1	tsp chopped fresh ginger root
¼	tsp ground black pepper
1	Tbsp thai or lemon basil
½	cup split mung beans
1½	cups water

Here's how:

Heat the ghee in a pot over medium heat. Then, add salt, sea palm, ginger and black pepper and simmer until the aroma comes up to meet you. Next add basil and simmer until the aroma is present. Add split mung beans; stir to coat with ghee and spices and simmer for a few minutes. Add water, stir and bring to a boil; reduce to simmer and cover for 25 minutes (stc), or 18 minutes (pc), allowing the pressure cooker to release naturally. Let sit 5 minutes after cooking, stir and serve warm.

Recipe 96 *(Warming)*

You'll need:

1-2	Tbsp ghee
⅓	tsp mineral salt
3	finger length stalks of lemongrass slit open
½	tsp cardamom seeds
¼	tsp ground black pepper
½	tsp asafoetida
½	cup split mung beans
2	cups water

Here's how:

Heat the ghee in a pot over medium heat. Then, add salt, lemongrass, cardamom and black pepper and simmer until the aroma comes up to meet you. Next add asafoetida and simmer until the aroma is present. Add split mung beans; stir to coat with ghee and spices and simmer for a few minutes. Add water, stir and bring to a boil; reduce to simmer and cover for 25 minutes (stc), or 18 minutes (pc), allowing the pressure cooker to release naturally. Let sit 5 minutes after cooking, stir and serve warm.

Recipe 97 *(Warming)*

You'll need:

1-2	Tbsp ghee
¾	tsp mineral salt
½	tsp fenugreek powder
1	tsp cardamom powder
¼	tsp ground black pepper
1	tsp dried lemongrass
½	cup split mung beans
2	cups water

Here's how:

Heat the ghee in a pot over medium heat. Then, add salt, fenugreek, cardamom and black pepper and simmer until the aroma comes up to meet you. Next add lemongrass and simmer until the aroma is present. Add split mung beans; stir to coat with ghee and spices and simmer for a few minutes. Add water, stir and bring to a boil; reduce to simmer and cover for 25 minutes (stc), or 18 minutes (pc), allowing the pressure cooker to release naturally. Let sit 5 minutes after cooking, stir and serve warm.

Recipe 98 *(Cooling)*

You'll need:

1	Tbsp sunflower oil
1	Tbsp ghee
⅓	tsp mineral salt
1	tsp fresh chopped ginger root
½	tsp fennel powder
1	tsp coriander powder
½	tsp spearmint leaves
½	cup split mung beans
2	cups water
¼	cup chopped fresh cilantro

Here's how:

Heat the ghee and oil in a pot over medium heat. Then, add salt, ginger, fennel and coriander and simmer until the aroma comes up to meet you. Next add spearmint and simmer until the aroma is present. Add split mung beans; stir to coat with ghee, oil and spices and simmer for a few minutes. Add water, stir and bring to a boil; reduce to simmer and cover for 25 minutes (stc), or 18 minutes (pc), allowing the pressure cooker to release naturally. Open and sprinkle on cilantro. Let sit 5 minutes after cooking, stir and serve warm.

Recipe 99 *(Warming)*

You'll need:

1-2	Tbsp ghee
⅓	tsp mineral salt
1	tsp cumin powder
1	tsp coriander powder
½	tsp asafoetida powder
1	Tbsp fresh dill
½	cup split mung beans
1½	cups water

Here's how:

Heat the ghee in a pot over medium heat. Then, add salt, cumin, coriander and asafoetida and simmer until the aroma comes up to meet you. Next add dill and simmer until the aroma is present. Add split mung beans; stir to coat with ghee and spices and simmer for a few minutes. Add water, stir and bring to a boil; reduce to simmer and cover for 25 minutes (stc), or 18 minutes (pc), allowing the pressure cooker to release naturally. Let sit 5 minutes after cooking, stir and serve warm.

Recipe 100 *(Warming)*

You'll need:

1-2	Tbsp ghee
⅓	tsp mineral salt
1	tsp fresh grated ginger root
1	tiny pinch red chilis
½	tsp mustard seeds
½	tsp turmeric powder
1	tsp dried thai basil
½	cup split mung beans
2	cups water

Here's how:

Heat the ghee in a pot over medium heat. Then, add salt, ginger, chilis and mustard seeds and simmer until the aroma comes up to meet you. Next add turmeric and basil and simmer until the aroma is present. Add split mung beans; stir to coat with ghee and spices and simmer for a few minutes. Add water, stir and bring to a boil; reduce to simmer and cover for 25 minutes (stc), or 18 minutes (pc), allowing the pressure cooker to release naturally. Let sit 5 minutes after cooking, stir and serve warm.

Recipe 101 *(Warming)*

You'll need:

1-2	Tbsp ghee
⅓	tsp mineral salt
1	tsp fresh chopped ginger root
1	tsp fresh chopped turmeric root
1	tsp cumin powder
1	tsp coriander powder
1	tsp dried lemongrass
½	cup whole mung beans
Water	

Here's how:

Heat the ghee in a pot over medium heat. Then, add salt, ginger and turmeric and simmer until the aroma comes up to meet you. Next add coriander and lemongrass and simmer until the aroma is present. Add whole mung beans; stir to coat with ghee and spices and simmer for a few minutes. Add water to cover, stir and bring to a boil; reduce to simmer and cover for 35 - 40 minutes (stc), or 25 minutes (pc), allowing the pressure cooker to release naturally. Let sit 5 minutes after cooking, stir and serve warm.

Recipe 102 *(Warming)*

You'll need:

2	Tbsp sunflower oil
⅓	tsp mineral salt
½	tsp fenugreek powder
1	tsp coriander powder
¼	tsp ground black pepper
1	tsp dried lemongrass
½	cup split mung beans
1½	cups water

Here's how:

Heat the oil in a pot over medium heat. Then, add salt, fenugreek, coriander and black pepper and simmer until the aroma comes up to meet you. Next add lemongrass and simmer until the aroma is present. Add split mung beans; stir to coat with oil and spices and simmer for a few minutes. Add water, stir and bring to a boil; reduce to simmer and cover for 25 minutes (stc), or 18 minutes (pc), allowing the pressure cooker to release naturally. Let sit 5 minutes after cooking, stir and serve warm.

Recipe 103 *(Warming)*

You'll need:

1-2	Tbsp ghee
⅓	tsp mineral salt
½	tsp dill seed
½	tsp cumin seed
1	tsp fennel powder
¼	cup fresh cilantro
½	cup whole mung beans
2	cups water

Here's how:

Heat the ghee in a pot over medium heat. Then, add salt, dill and cumin and simmer until the aroma comes up to meet you. Next add fennel and most of the cilantro and simmer until the aroma is present. Add whole mung beans; stir to coat with ghee and spices and simmer for a few minutes. Add water to cover, stir and bring to a boil; reduce to simmer and cover for 35 - 40 minutes (stc), or 25 minutes (pc), allowing the pressure cooker to release naturally. Open and sprinkle a bit of the cilantro on top. Let sit 5 minutes after cooking, stir and serve warm.

Recipe 104 *(Warming -)*

You'll need:

1-2	Tbsp ghee
⅓	tsp mineral salt
1	Tbsp seaweed
1	tsp coriander powder
½	tsp fenugreek powder
½	tsp dried peppermint
1	tsp dried lemongrass
½	cup split mung beans
2	cups water

Here's how:

Heat the ghee in a pot over medium heat. Then, add salt, seaweed, coriander and fenugreek and simmer until the aroma comes up to meet you. Next add peppermint and lemongrass and simmer until the aroma is present. Add split mung beans; stir to coat with ghee and spices and simmer for a few minutes. Add water, stir and bring to a boil; reduce to simmer and cover for 25 minutes (stc), or 18 minutes (pc), allowing the pressure cooker to release naturally. Let sit 5 minutes after cooking, stir and serve warm.

Recipe 105 *(Warming +)*

You'll need:

1-2	Tbsp	ghee
⅓	tsp	mineral salt
½	tsp	ground cumin seeds
½	tsp	ground fennel seeds
½	tsp	anise seeds
¾	tsp	ginger powder
¼	tsp	dried peppermint
½	cup	split mung beans
2	cups	water

Here's how:

Heat the ghee in a pot over medium heat. Then, add salt, cumin, fennel and anise seeds and simmer until the aroma comes up to meet you. Next add ginger and peppermint and simmer until the aroma is present. Add split mung beans; stir to coat with ghee and spices and simmer for a few minutes. Add water, stir and bring to a boil; reduce to simmer and cover for 25 minutes (stc), or 18 minutes (pc), allowing the pressure cooker to release naturally. Let sit 5 minutes after cooking, stir and serve warm.

Recipe 106 *(Cooling)*

You'll need:

1	Tbsp	ghee
1	Tbsp	coconut oil
⅓	tsp	mineral salt
½	tsp	ground coriander seeds
1	tsp	fresh cilantro
1	tsp	fresh mint
½	cup	split mung beans
1½	cups	water

Here's how:

Heat the ghee and oil in a pot over medium heat. Then, add salt and coriander and simmer until the aroma comes up to meet you. Next add cilantro and mint and simmer until the aroma is present. Add split mung beans; stir to coat with ghee and spices and simmer for a few minutes. Add water, stir and bring to a boil; reduce to simmer and cover for 25 minutes (stc), or 18 minutes (pc), allowing the pressure cooker to release naturally. Let sit 5 minutes after cooking, stir and serve warm.

Recipe 107 *(Warming)*

You'll need:

1-2	Tbsp ghee
⅓	tsp mineral salt
1	tsp seaweed
½	tsp mustard seeds
½	tsp anise seeds
1	tsp fresh mint leaves
½	cup split mung beans
1½	cups water

Here's how:

Heat the ghee in a pot over medium heat. Then, add salt, seaweed, mustard and anise seeds and simmer until the aroma comes up to meet you. Next add mint and simmer until the aroma is present. Add split mung beans; stir to coat with ghee and spices and simmer for a few minutes. Add water, stir and bring to a boil; reduce to simmer and cover for 25 minutes (stc), or 18 minutes (pc), allowing the pressure cooker to release naturally. Let sit 5 minutes after cooking, stir and serve warm.

Recipe 108 *(Warming)*

You'll need:

1-2	Tbsp ghee
⅓	tsp mineral salt
1	tsp seaweed
2	star anise
½	tsp cinnamon powder
½	tsp black pepper
1	tbsp fresh dill
½	cup split mung beans
1½	cups water

Here's how:

Heat the ghee in a pot over medium heat. Then, add salt, seaweed, and anise and simmer until the aroma comes up to meet you. Next add cinnamon, black pepper, and 1 tsp dill and simmer until the aroma is present. Add split mung beans; stir to coat with ghee and spices and simmer for a few minutes. Add water, stir and bring to a boil; reduce to simmer and cover for 25 minutes (stc), or 18 minutes (pc), allowing the pressure cooker to release naturally. Open and add the additional dill. Let sit 5 minutes after cooking, stir and serve warm.

<u>*The end of the beginning*</u>

I hope these 108 recipes will provide you with many choices and stimulate you to develop your own creations each day based on the principles of Ayurveda.

When preparing a meal, consider the heating and cooling qualities of the spices, the quantity of each spice, and the weather. Recognize how the food you eat can provide balance to your body and mind.

The sacred nature of eating is so integral to our experience of life. It affects our mental and emotional state, our spiritual connection as well as the physical body. Bring an attitude of respect, creativity and love to your food preparation and to the eating process. Work with your intuition to bring balance to your cooking, which in turn will bring balance to your eating and your life. No matter where you are in your life, you have the opportunity to learn what it means to feed yourself at the deepest level. It is an act of love. When you regard eating as a sacred act, you will experience satisfaction deeply with every meal, and all parts of life.

We have many other recipes on our website, halepule.com, and we offer Ayurveda trainings, consultations, and mentoring as well as authentic Ayurvedic treatment for disease prevention and reversal. Join us in life's journey with Ayurveda.

Index

Recipes by virya

Virya (feeling of warming/cooling in stomach and small intestines).
• Cooling
• Neutral
• Warming -
• Warming
• Warming +

The virya (warming, cooling, or neutral quality) of the dhal is indicated for each recipe. The degree of the warming and cooling nature is expressed with "+" or "-" after the word warming or cooling for each recipe. Choose your recipe each day based on how you feel inside, the weather outside, and what you have available. Use the principle of opposite qualities bring balance. If you feel hot inside your body then choose a cooling or neutral recipe to support digestion and help to balance dosha. If you feel cool inside your body then choose a warming recipe. Use the more warming recipes on a chilly day, and use the more cooling recipes in warm to hot weather. In hot weather, it's also a good idea to reduce the amount of spicing by to proportionately to better support agni, which naturally lowers in hot weather to help the body stay cool.

Cooling

Neutral

Warming –

- Recipe 5 - Dhal (Chinese-inspired)
- Recipe 6 - Dhal (Chinese-inspired)
- Recipe 9 - Dhal (Indian-inspired)
- Recipe 30 - Complete balance bowl (Japanese-inspired)
- Recipe 57 - Dhal (Middle Eastern-inspired)
- Recipe 59 - Dhal (Middle Eastern-inspired)
- Recipe 30 - Complete balance bowl (Mediterranean-inspired)
- Recipe 83 - Complete balance bowl (Mexican-inspired)
- Recipe 88 - Dhal (Mexican-inspired)
- Recipe 93 - Complete balance bowl (New Zealand-inspired)
- Recipe 104 - Dhal (Vietnamese-inspired)

Warming

- Recipe 3 - Dhal (Chinese-inspired)
- Recipe 4 - Dhal (Chinese-inspired)
- Recipe 12 - Dhal (Indian-inspired)
- Recipe 13 - Dhal (Indian-inspired)
- Recipe 15 - Dhal (Indian-inspired)
- Recipe 18 - Dhal (Indian-inspired)
- Recipe 19 - Dhal (Indian-inspired)
- Recipe 23 - Dhal (Indian-inspired)
- Recipe 31 - Dhal (Japanese-inspired)
- Recipe 33 - Dhal (Japanese-inspired)
- Recipe 34 - Dhal (Japanese-inspired)
- Recipe 37 - Dhal (Japanese-inspired)
- Recipe 39 - Dhal (Japanese-inspired)
- Recipe 40 - Dhal (Japanese-inspired)
- Recipe 42 - Dhal (Japanese-inspired)
- Recipe 44 - Dhal (Middle Eastern-inspired)

- Recipe 45 - Dhal (Middle Eastern-inspired)
- Recipe 46 - Dhal (Middle Eastern-inspired)
- Recipe 47 - Dhal (Middle Eastern-inspired)
- Recipe 48 - Dhal (Middle Eastern-inspired)
- Recipe 49 - Dhal (Middle Eastern-inspired)
- Recipe 50 - Dhal (Middle Eastern-inspired)
- Recipe 51 - Dhal (Middle Eastern-inspired)
- Recipe 52 - Dhal (Middle Eastern-inspired)
- Recipe 53 - Dhal (Middle Eastern-inspired)
- Recipe 54 - Dhal (Middle Eastern-inspired)
- Recipe 55 - Dhal (Middle Eastern-inspired)
- Recipe 58 - Dhal (Middle Eastern-inspired)
- Recipe 64 - Dhal (Mediterranean-inspired)
- Recipe 65 - Dhal (Mediterranean-inspired)
- Recipe 66 - Dhal (Mediterranean-inspired)
- Recipe 67 - Dhal (Mediterranean-inspired)
- Recipe 72 - Dhal (Mediterranean-inspired)
- Recipe 73 - Dhal (Mediterranean-inspired)
- Recipe 74 - Dhal (Mediterranean-inspired)
- Recipe 75 - Dhal (Mediterranean-inspired)
- Recipe 76 - Dhal (Mediterranean-inspired)
- Recipe 77 - Dhal (Mediterranean-inspired)
- Recipe 84 - Dhal (Mexican-inspired)
- Recipe 85 - Dhal (Mexican-inspired)
- Recipe 86 - Dhal (Mexican-inspired)
- Recipe 87 - Dhal (Mexican-inspired)
- Recipe 89 - Dhal (Mexican-inspired)
- Recipe 95 - Dhal (Vietnamese-inspired)
- Recipe 96 - Dhal (Vietnamese-inspired)
- Recipe 97 - Dhal (Vietnamese-inspired)
- Recipe 99 - Dhal (Vietnamese-inspired)
- Recipe 101 - Dhal (Vietnamese-inspired)
- Recipe 102 - Dhal (Vietnamese-inspired)
- Recipe 103 - Dhal (Vietnamese-inspired)
- Recipe 107 - Dhal (Vietnamese-inspired)
- Recipe 108 - Dhal (Vietnamese-inspired)

Warming +

- Recipe 1 - Complete balance bowl (Chinese-inspired)
- Recipe 2 - Dhal (Chinese-inspired)
- Recipe 7 - Dhal (Chinese-inspired)
- Recipe 8 - Complete balance bowl (Indian-inspired)
- Recipe 10 - Dhal (Indian-inspired)
- Recipe 11 - Dhal (Indian-inspired)
- Recipe 14 - Dhal (Indian-inspired)
- Recipe 16 - Dhal (Indian-inspired)
- Recipe 17 - Dhal (Indian-inspired)
- Recipe 20 - Dhal (Indian-inspired)

- Recipe 21 - Dhal (Indian-inspired)
- Recipe 25 - Dhal (Indian-inspired)
- Recipe 29 - Dhal (Indian-inspired)
- Recipe 36 - Dhal (Japanese-inspired)
- Recipe 41 - Dhal (Japanese-inspired)
- Recipe 56 - Dhal (Middle Eastern-inspired)
- Recipe 68 - Dhal (Mediterranean-inspired)
- Recipe 69 - Dhal (Mediterranean-inspired)
- Recipe 70 - Dhal (Mediterranean-inspired)
- Recipe 71 - Dhal (Mediterranean-inspired)
- Recipe 78 - Dhal (Mediterranean-inspired)
- Recipe 100 - Dhal (Vietnamese-inspired)
- Recipe 105 - Dhal (Vietnamese-inspired)

Appendix

Augmenting and extractive foods

This augmenting and extractive food list is not intended to be comprehensive and not all foods listed are recommended for all people. Rather, the lists are designed to give you a sense of the qualities of different foods. If a particular food is not listed here, consider how it tastes. Remember, augmenting foods are primarily sweet in taste, while extractive foods are more bitter, pungent, and/or astringent. Enjoy a ratio of 60% augmenting to 40% extractive foods as part of a balanced, nourishing meal.

Augmenting foods

Grains:
Amaranth
Barley
Buckwheat
Bulgur wheat
Farro
Millet
Mochi (fresh)
Quinoa
Rice - brown, white, other
Rye
Soba (fresh)
Steel cut oats
Teff
Udon (fresh)
Wheat
Wild rice

Vegetables:
Beets
Breadfruit
Carrots
Cassava
Chayote
Corn
Cucumber
Daikon - sweet
Fennel root
Lotus root
Parsnips
Rutabaga
Salsify
Squash (kabocha, acorn, spaghetti, butternut, pumpkin)
Sweet potatoes
Taro
Tigernut
Turnips - sweet
Yacon
Yams
Zucchini

Dairy:
Organic, fresh, raw is best
Buttermilk
Ghee
Fresh goat cheese
Fresh farmer's cheese
Fresh mozzarella
Fresh yogurt
Paneer
Raw or non-homogenized milk

Fruits
(fresh and dried):
Apples
Apricots
Bananas
Berries
Cherimoya
Cherries
Chico
Cranberries
Currants
Dates
Dragonfruit
Figs
Grapefruit
Grapes - with seeds
Guava
Jackfruit
Kiwifruit
Kumquat
Lemons
Limes
Longan
Lychee
Mango
Melons
Mulberry
Nectarines
Oranges
Papayas
Passionfruit
Peaches
Pears
Persimmon
Plum
Pineapples
Pomegranates
Prunes
Raisins
Sapote
Starfruit
Strawberries

Other:
Avocados
Sea vegetables

Extractive foods

Legumes:	Nuts and seeds:	Vegetables:	
Anasazi	Almonds	Artichoke	Daikon - pungent
Adzuki	Brazil nuts	Asparagus	Drumstick
Black-eyed peas	Cashews	Bamboo shoot	Fiddlehead ferns
Black lentils	Chia seeds	Beet greens	Kale
Brown lentils	Coconut	Bitter gourd	Kohlrabi
Chana dhal	Fennel seeds	Bok choy	Mustard greens
Garbanzos	Flax seeds	Broccoli	Okra
Green beans	Gingko nuts	Brussels sprouts	Peas
Green lentils	Hazelnuts	Burdock root	Plantain
Lima beans	Macadamia	Cabbage	Spinach
Mung beans	Pistachio	Cauliflower	Swiss chard
Toor dhal	Pecans	Celery	Tatsoi
Tofu (non-GMO)	Pine nuts	Celery root	Wasabi
Red lentils	Pumpkin seeds	Chinese cabbage	Water chesnut
Snow cap beans	Sesame seeds	Collards	Watercress
Soybean (non-GMO)	Sunflower seeds	Dandelion leaf	
Split mung beans			
Split peas			
Urud dhal			
Wing beans			

Appendix

The use of spices and herbs is a way to support digestion, balance the qualities in a meal and enhance the taste of the food. Since rasa (taste), virya heating or cooling, and vipaka post-digestive, are somewhat subjective your experience may differ from what you read here.

It is important to recognize that we are referring to the moderate use of spices. Often the effects will change when used in large amounts. **Moderation is the key and more is not better.** Use the spices to uplift the taste of the food and no one spice should stand out. Allow them all to become friends. Value your experience and let us know how it goes by emailing info@halepule.com.

Ajwain is Indian celery seed. It is bitter and pungent, has warming virya and pungent vipaka. A little goes a long way.

Allspice is sweet and pungent. It has warming virya and pungent vipaka.

Anise seed is sweet. It has warming virya and sweet vipaka, aids digestion, supports agni, breaks up mucus, calms the mind for sleep, and supports heart health. Star anise is considered more potent.

Asafoetida, also called hing, is pungent. It has warming virya and pungent vipaka. It is a digestive aid and dispels gas and cramping, destroys parasites, and cleanses the intestinal tract. Use in small amounts as it is rajasic. Avoid asafoetida with chemical preservatives.

Basil, fresh or dried, is pungent, has warming virya and pungent vipaka. Tulsi basil is said to be less heating than Italian basil and sattvic.

Bay leaves are pungent, has warming virya and pungent vipaka. They are stimulating, extractive and support digestion.

Black pepper is pungent, bitter and sweet, has heating virya and pungent vipaka. It increases pitta and decreases vata and kapha. It destroys digestive toxins and stimulates agni.

Cardamom is sweet and pungent. Some say it is cooling and some say warming. Perhaps cooling in seed form and warming as a powder. Sweet vipaka can be experienced in pod, seed, or powder form. Reduce mucus formation, stimulates agni, balances all doshas, increases joy and vitality in the body, calms nausea and detoxifies caffeine.

Carob is slightly sweet and bitter. It has warming virya and pungent vipaka. It is a great caffeine free alternative to cacao.

Cayenne is pungent. It has heating virya and pungent vipaka. It easily aggravates pitta. Black pepper and pippali are preferred in Ayurveda.

Celery seed (western) is sweet and astringent. It has cooling virya and sweet vipaka.

Chili peppers are pungent. They have heating virya and pungent vipaka. They may be used in small amounts on occasion when pitta is in balance.

Chives are pungent. They have warming virya and pungent vipaka. They are rajasic and aggravate the digestive tract and overstimulate the mind.

Cilantro is pungent and sweet. It has cooling virya and pungent vipaka. It is stimulating and has diuretic qualities, balances pitta, and reduces the effects of radiation.

Cinnamon is sweet, pungent, and astringent. It has warming virya and sweet vipaka, augmenting, decreases vata and kapha and increases pitta. Cinnamon strengthens and harmonizes circulation, the heart and the kidneys, is stimulating and has diuretic qualities.

Cloves are pungent and bitter. They have warming virya and sweet vipaka. Cloves are augmenting, aid digestion, dispel gas and reduce congestion.

Coriander is pungent, sweet and bitter. It has cooling virya and pungent vipaka, extractive, dispels gas and bloating. It is stimulating, aids digestion, is excellent for balancing the urinary tract and balances all doshas.

Cumin is pungent and bitter. It has warming virya and pungent vipaka. It dispels and counters gas, supports digestion, and balances all doshas, especially vata and kapha.

Curry leaf is sweet and pungent. It has warming virya and pungent vipaka, supports agni and removing toxins.

Curry powder is a pre-mixed blend of spices. It is typically coriander, turmeric, cumin, fenugreek, chili peppers and asafoetida, and oftentimes others. To better regulate the amount of pungency and warming virya in meals, we suggest to use the spices individually rather than in the pre-mixed curry powder form.

Dandelion leaf is bitter, astringent and pungent. It was warming virya and pungent vipaka. It is diuretic and cleanses the kidneys, liver and gallbladder.

Dill can be in fresh leaf, dried leaf or seed form, and is pungent. The leaf is cooling and the seed is warming while the vipaka of both is pungent. It is stimulating.

Fennel is pungent, sweet and bitter. The seed and powder are warming while the fresh root is less so. Some say fennel has cooling virya. It has sweet vipaka and is great for cleansing the kidneys, supporting digestion and reducing gas.

Fenugreek is pungent, astringent, sweet and bitter. It has heating virya and pungent vipaka. It is a digestive aid, decreases vata and kapha and increases pitta. Fenugreek is stimulating and rejuvenates and tones the entire body.

Garlic is primarily pungent and sweet. It has all other tastes in moderation except salty. It has heating virya and aggravates the digestive tract blocking the flow of energy, which outweighs isolated benefits. It has pungent vipaka. It reduces ama in small amounts. It is not recommended in Ayurveda nor Yoga.

Ginger is pungent and sweet. It has neutral to warming virya in moderate amounts and sweet vipaka. Good quality fresh ginger has five of the six tastes, except salty. Vipaka is sweet although pungent in too large quantity.

Dried ginger powder has pungent vipaka. Fresh ginger is sattvic and balancing for all doshas in moderate amounts, especially vata and kapha. Ginger relieves gas, cramps and nausea, stimulates the appetite and digests toxins in the body.

Hibiscus is sour and bitter. It has cooling virya and sweet vipaka. It balances pitta and prevents balding, anemia, reduces swelling and inflammation and supports balanced mental function.

Kafir lime leaves provide bitter and sour taste. They have warming virya and pungent vipaka. They are used as digestive support and provide balance to a dish.

Lemongrass is sour with some bitter and sour vipaka. It has extractive qualities and supports the balance of a meal.

Lemon peel or zest is bitter, sour and astringent. It has warming virya and pungent vipaka.

Marjoram is pungent and bitter. It has warming virya and pungent vipaka, stimulates digestion, cleanses the spleen, burns toxins, and promotes circulation. In excess it is drying.

Mint is pungent. It has cooling virya in small amounts, and pungent vipaka. In excess it becomes heating. Mint, including peppermint and spearmint, is stimulating and calms nausea.

Moringa is pungent and bitter. It has warming virya and pungent vipaka, stimulates digestion, promotes dryness, balances vata and kapha, supports heart health and detoxifies the tissues of the body.

Mustard seeds are pungent and bitter. They have heating virya and pungent vipaka, oily, stimulating, aid digestion, dispel gas and toxins and stimulate circulation. Mustard seeds assist the digestion of protein. Yellow mustard seeds are more pungent than brown or black.

Nutmeg is pungent, bitter and astringent. It has warming virya and pungent vipaka, calming, has sedative qualities and supports improved absorption.

Onion is sweet and pungent. It has warming virya and pungent vipaka. Some say it has sweet vipaka. It can be detoxifying in small amounts and is an aphrodisiac. It increases rajas, over stimulation in the mind, and aggravates the digestive tract. It is not recommended in Ayurveda nor Yoga.

Oregano is pungent. It has warming virya and pungent vipaka. Oregano is drying, stimulating and calms nausea, gas and indigestion.

Paprika is pungent. It has warming virya and pungent vipaka, less heating than cayenne and in moderation can reduce vata and kapha. It increases circulation, detoxifies and increases pitta.

Parsley is pungent and astringent. It has cooling virya and pungent vipaka. Parsley is stimulating and has diuretic qualities. It calms edema and cleanses rakta.

Poppyseed is sweet and bitter. It has warming virya and sweet vipaka. It is tranquilizing and relaxing.

Rosemary is pungent. It has warming virya and pungent vipaka. It is dry and stimulating.

Rosehips are astringent, pungent and sour. They have warming virya and pungent vipaka. They enhance immunity, are mild diuretics and laxatives, and cleanse the kidneys.

Rose petals are bitter and astringent. They have cooling virya and pungent vipaka. They can be used fresh or dried if they are organically grown without pesticides, herbicides or chemical fertilizers. Rose petals cleanse the skin and reduce pitta.

Saffron is pungent with some bitter and sweet rasa. It has a slightly warming virya and pungent vipaka. It enhances the effects of other spices and food. It supports the assimilation of nutrients into the tissues of the body, balances all doshas and is a digestive aid. Saffron builds blood and regulates the menstrual cycle, and increases love, devotion and compassion.

Sage is pungent and astringent. It has warming virya and pungent vipaka, drying, stimulating and has diuretic qualities. It helps clear the energy channelsi.

Salt is salty and pungent. It has warming virya and sweet vipaka. Moderate use in cooking helps balance vata dosha. Without salt vata increases so it is necessary and balancing in moderate amounts. Mineral salt or rock salt from the earth is best. Salt added after cooking is too strong and not recommended. Cooking salt into food helps soften it for digestion and promotes absorption of water into the food.

Sansho is pungent and sour. It has a warming virya and pungent vipak. This Japanese pepper has a citrus flavor and stimulates agni.

Shiso is bitter, pungent and astringent with a little sweet, has warming virya and pungent vipaka.

Tamarind is sour. It has warming virya and sour vipaka and is a good replacement for vinegar.

Thyme is pungent. It has warming virya and pungent vipaka, is dry, stimulating and antiseptic.

Tarragon is pungent and astringent, and has warming virya and pungent vipaka. It is dry, promotes circulation and supports lymphatic drainage.

Turmeric is bitter, pungent and astringent. It has warming virya and pungent vipaka. In moderation it balances all doshas. Turmeric in moderation is stimulating and purifying for the blood, mind and skin. It is a natural antibiotic and strengthens intestinal flora, cleanses the energetic channels and restores ligaments. Turmeric helps digest protein and promotes balanced metabolism.

Vanilla bean is sweet. It has cooling virya and sweet vipaka. It is sattvic and grounding and balances vata and pitta.

Wasabi is pungent, bitter and a little sweet when pure. It has warming virya and pungent vipaka. Fresh wasabi root is mild unlike most pastes or powders.

Made in the USA
Monee, IL
26 October 2024

68699249R00076